"THE WAVE IS CRASHING: WILL W
This book is, in effect, a crash course for swimmin
can survive the confluence of economic crisis, clim
overpopulation, and all the rest—but not without profoundly changing the ways
we think, relate to one another, and treat our environment. *The Great Waves of
Change* tells us how."

RICHARD HEINBERG
Author of *The Party's Over*
Senior Fellow, Post Carbon Institute

"Marshall Summers' work provides an outline of the coming changes and
prepares the reader for living in a radically different world."

GEORGE NOORY
National Talk Show Host, Coast To Coast AM

"In this powerful and practical book, Marshall Vian Summers has painstakingly
shown us the urgency of preparing spiritually for the daunting, unprecedented
changes that lie ahead—the dire consequences of not doing so and the profound
transformation of the human species that is likely to occur if we do."

CAROLYN BAKER, PH.D.
Author of *Sacred Demise: Walking The Spiritual Path of Industrial Civilization's Collapse*
Publisher of Speaking Truth to Power

"Summers has written an engaging, spiritual challenge for all people who seek to
resolve broad-ranging conflicts, engage life according to a true moral compass,
and seek innovative ways to reconcile the individual with the sacred Earth, of
which we are all a part."

MICHAEL TOBIAS
Author of *A Vision of Nature: Traces of the Original World*

"Marshall Vian Summers has accomplished a brilliant piece of work. It is an
experience just to sit down and read it. You really do feel moved to assess where
you are in life. You feel called upon to ask the difficult inquiry of yourself, 'Is
this really the direction I want to be moving?' There were parts as I was moving
through the book I just wanted to shut it, I didn't want to hear it, but I knew it
was a great challenge to seek deep within oneself and ask those difficult
questions concerning what road I will choose to travel. *The Great Waves of
Change* is written for everyone."

NOVEMBER HANSON
Voice of the People Radio

OTHER WRITINGS

by

MARSHALL VIAN SUMMERS

Steps to Knowledge

Greater Community Spirituality

Wisdom from the Greater Community:
Volumes I & II

The Allies of Humanity:
Books One & Two

Relationships and Higher Purpose

Living the Way of Knowledge

THE
GREAT
WAVES OF
CHANGE

Navigating the
Difficult Times Ahead

MARSHALL VIAN SUMMERS

New
Knowledge
Library

THE GREAT WAVES OF CHANGE: *Navigating the Difficult Times Ahead*

Copyright © 2009 by The Society for The Greater Community Way of Knowledge. Printed and bound in the United States of America. All rights reserved.

Great Waves storm image by John Lund
Book design by Argent Associates, Boulder, Colorado

ISBN: 978-1-884238-60-4

Library of Congress Control Number: 2009924308

Publisher's Cataloging-in-Publication
(Provided by Quality Books, Inc.)

Summers, Marshall Vian.
   The great waves of change : navigating the difficult
times ahead / Marshall Vian Summers.
   p. cm.
   LCCN 2009924308
   ISBN-13: 978-1-884238-60-4
   ISBN-10: 1-884238-60-2

   1. Spiritual life—Society for The Greater Community
Way of Knowledge. 2. History, Modern—21st century.
3. Change. 4. Change (Psychology)—Religious aspects.
5. Society for The Greater Community Way of Knowledge.
I. Title.

BP605.S58S825 2009   299´.93
                                    QBI09-600036

The books of New Knowledge Library are published by The Society for The Greater Community Way of Knowledge, a non-profit organization.

THE GREAT WAVES OF CHANGE is part of a larger teaching representing a New Message for Humanity. Formal study of the New Message is presented in the texts GREATER COMMUNITY SPIRITUALITY, STEPS TO KNOWLEDGE and WISDOM FROM THE GREATER COMMUNITY: *Volumes I & II*, which can be requested at your local bookstore and library, ordered online or ordered directly from The Society.

To order the books of the New Knowledge Library or to receive information about The Society's audio recordings, educational programs and contemplative services, please visit The Society's Homepage on the World Wide Web, or contact:

The Society for The Greater Community Way of Knowledge
P.O. Box 1724 • Boulder, CO 80306-1724 • (303) 938-8401
society@greatercommunity.org
www.greatwavesofchange.org

*For one who has perception,
a mere sign is enough.*

*For one who does not heed,
a thousand explanations
are not enough.*

HAJJI BEKTASH WALI
Persian Mystic
1209-1271

Contents

Introduction

HUMANITY HAS CROSSED A CRITICAL THRESHOLD where we will have to adapt to a whole new set of circumstances. This will require a united effort between governments and peoples to bring new levels of skill, technology and cooperation to meet the requirements of living in a radically changing world.

At the core of this united effort are the courage and the ability within people to see what is coming, to know what to do and to act wisely in the face of increasing uncertainty and upheaval. Nature has given us this courage and this set of abilities, but they have become latent and forgotten within the human family. More than anything else, it is these abilities that will determine how, and even if, humanity will prepare for the Great Waves of change and the kind of world we will all have to face as a result.

In facing the Great Waves of change, preparation is the key. The preparation is not merely about fortifying your outer life or attempting to build a sustainable lifestyle. Instead, it is about preparing for a whole new reality. This new reality will require that you become self-reliant and able to call upon a deeper strength within yourself and within others, a strength that few people are yet aware of. This strength is within you now and has been with you all along. This book will reveal to you where it can be found and how it can be used.

The preparation begins with what you see in the world and what you are aware of within yourself. As you proceed, the preparation strengthens your ability to be perceptive, resourceful and wise in responding to changing and unpredictable circumstances.

If you can recognize the reality and the power of the Great Waves to impact your life, this will naturally begin a long process of re-evaluation regarding how you live, where you live, your use of resources, the strength or weakness of your relationships in helping you to prepare and the direction your life really needs to follow.

In facing great change and uncertainty, particularly if it has not been anticipated, people do not rely upon logic and reason as much as upon assumptions, habits and the behavior of the people around them. This is why the inner preparation is so important. Without this inner preparation, people will tend to wait until the last moment to react when their options will be few, if any. When many people respond in this way, there is chaos.

We each have a greater intelligence within us called Knowledge that is not afraid of the future or the challenge of changing our lives. This native intelligence has the power to move us or to restrain us when necessary and to enable us to find the people and the opportunities that hold the greatest promise for our lives. The significance, power and application of this greater intelligence go far beyond our notions of intuition and instinct. Here the Great Waves of change, though dangerous and largely unforeseen, hold the ultimate opportunity for those who can prepare to reclaim this deeper intelligence to secure their lives and to find their unique contribution to a world in need.

Here you will find, presented in the most clear and uncompromising manner, the gravity of the Great Waves of change and the kinds of fundamental decisions each of us will have to face and to make if we are to wisely prepare. There are two minds within us: a worldly mind that is shaped by the prevailing beliefs and attitudes of our families and culture and a deeper, more powerful mind that is free from these influences. Which voice within us we respond to and choose to follow will make all the difference in our ability to see, to know and to act wisely when others around us seem unable or unwilling to do so.

This book confronts us with dangerous scenarios that are the logical outcome of our collective failure to respond adequately to the Great Waves of change that are already beginning to impact our world. It speaks to the fundamental question, "How will you know what to do in the difficult times ahead?" Governments cannot tell you. Scientists cannot tell you. Religious leaders cannot tell you. How will you answer this question for yourself? This book shows you how.

The message of THE GREAT WAVES OF CHANGE is direct and challenging. Its assault upon human ignorance, assumptions and arrogance is unrelenting. Yet this book gives us real vision about the kind of world we will have to face and where, above all other things, we will find the source of our strength, wisdom and courage to navigate the difficult times ahead. Those difficult times have now begun. The Great Waves of change are upon us.

MARSHALL VIAN SUMMERS
Seattle, 2009

CHAPTER 1

The Great Waves of Change

GREAT CHANGE IS COMING TO THE WORLD, change unlike anything that humanity as a whole has ever seen before—Great Waves of change all converging at this time. For humanity has impacted the world in so many ways, and the results of that impact are now gathering—gathering strength, gathering force, converging at a time when humanity is largely unaware and unprepared.

These Great Waves are not one event. They are not one simple thing that happens at one time only, for humanity has set in motion forces of change now that it must contend with on an ongoing basis. For you are now living in a world of declining resources, a world whose climate has been seriously affected, a world whose ecological condition is deteriorating, a world where humanity will have to face the prospects of great shortages of food and water and the risks of disease and illness on a very large scale, even affecting the wealthy nations of the world. The balance has now been tipped and changed, and the human family as a whole must unite and gather together to deal with these great challenges.

In a world of ever-growing population and declining resources, humanity will face a great decision, a fundamental choice in which direction to go. Do nations compete and challenge each other for the remaining resources? Do they fight and struggle over who will control these resources and who

1

will have access to these resources? For indeed, all the great wars of humanity's turbulent past have been a struggle, fundamentally, over gaining access to and control over resources.

Will the wealthy nations of the world insist that their lifestyle must be preserved and therefore enter into competition and conflict with one another, further degrading the rest of the world, robbing the poorer people of the world of their own ability to sustain themselves so that some grand or indulgent lifestyle can be maintained in the wealthy nations?

If humanity chooses this path, it will enter a period of prolonged conflict and permanent decline. Instead of preserving and distributing the remaining resources and generating the ability to adapt to a new world condition, humanity will destroy what is left, leaving itself poor and bereft, with immense loss of human life and with very grim and grave prospects for the future.

Yet if humanity chooses a different path, recognizing the inherent dangers involved in facing these Great Waves of change, recognizing the seriousness of their reality and the great consequences that they can have for the well-being and for the future of humanity, then wise individuals and leaders of nations and religious institutions can recognize that divided, humanity will fail in the face of the Great Waves of change. But united, humanity can chart a new course, prepare for the impacts of the Great Waves of change and set in course the beginnings of a greater cooperation and a greater unity than humanity as a whole has ever experienced before. This will be generated now not by religious principles or by high ethics, but by sheer necessity itself.

For what can one nation hope to achieve if the world plunges into conflict and deprivation? Nations of the world are far too interdependent now to choose the path of war and conflict without bringing ruin and deprivation to everyone.

United, you have a great chance. Divided, you will fail. And your failure will be longstanding, and it will be extremely costly—greater than any war that has ever occurred in this world will it be, more devastating than any human conflict that humanity has ever known.

The choices are few, but they are fundamental. And those choices must not be made simply by the leaders of nations and religious institutions, but by each citizen. Each person must choose whether they will fight and compete, whether they will resist the Great Waves of change, whether they will struggle with themselves and with others to maintain whatever lifestyle they are holding onto. Or will they recognize the great danger, and will they unite to begin to prepare for its impact and to build a new and different kind of future for humanity?

The first great challenge facing you is to face the great challenge.

For you cannot maintain the way you live now. Those rich nations, those wealthy people, those people who have become accustomed to affluence, feeling it is not only a right but an entitlement from God and from life—they must be prepared to change the way they live, to live far more simply, to live far more equitably, for the sharing of the remaining resources will require this.

The rich will have to take care of the poor, and the poor will have to take care of one another, or failure faces everyone, rich and poor. There will be no winners if human civilization should fail. There will be no supreme nations. There will be no supreme tribe or group or religious body if civilization fails. And the Great Waves of change have the power to lead human civilization to failure. That is how great they are. That is how long reaching their impact will be.

Therefore, the first great challenge facing you is to face the great challenge—without insisting upon solutions, without fighting against the truth of what you know and what you see, without blaming other people or expecting someone else to take care of the problem for you. Everyone must take responsibility in how they live, in how they think, in what they do, in the decisions before them today, and in the decisions that they will have to face in the future. Everyone, particularly those of the wealthy nations, will have to reconsider where they live, how they live, what kind of employment they have, how they make a living, how they use the resources of the world, how they use energy—all of these things.

Humanity has squandered its natural inheritance.

It is certainly not a time to be ambivalent or complacent. It is certainly not a time to just think that government leaders should take care of the problem for you, for you must now look to your life and to your circumstances.

It is as if the bill has come due. Humanity has been spending and borrowing its natural inheritance for so long, postponing the payment of the consequences of this for so long, and now the bill has come due. Now the consequences are emerging powerfully, and there are many of them.

Now you must reckon what you have created. You must reckon your condition. You must reckon your circumstances. You must reckon the world that you are creating for yourself. For humanity has squandered its natural inheritance. This abundant, magnificent world that the Creator of all life has given to humanity as its own world has been plundered and squandered and wasted—through greed, through corruption, through war and conflict, through irresponsible behavior, through unawareness and ignorance—and now the consequences are beginning to emerge. They are not simply a distant possibility or a problem for some future generation.

This is the world that you have come to serve. This is the world you have created. These are the circumstances facing you now. You must face them. You must take responsibility that you have played a small part in creating them. You must accept this responsibility without shame, but the responsibility is there nonetheless. For in the face of the Great Waves of change, there is nowhere to run and hide. You cannot simply pack your bags and move to the country or go find someplace to hide while the storm passes over, for this storm will last a long time, and there is nowhere to hide.

Only Knowledge within you, the deeper intelligence that God has placed within you, will know how to deal with these circumstances and with the immense change that is coming for humanity. Only this deeper Knowledge, this sacred Knowledge, will know how to navigate the difficult times ahead, will know how to sail the troubled waters, for troubled waters there will be.

Perhaps you are accustomed to being untroubled by the greater problems of the world. Perhaps you have insulated yourself sufficiently where they seem to be distant, where they do not seem to be a problem for you. They seem to be someone else's problem, a problem in another country, a problem that other people have to face and deal with. But such insulation now is over. It is not possible that you will not be greatly impacted by the Great Waves of change. It is not possible that they will not change your circumstances, perhaps even dramatically.

In essence, you cannot change what is coming now, but you can prepare for it. You can adapt to it. You can use it to contribute to the well-being of people, for this indeed is why you have come to the world. At a greater level, beyond your thoughts and beliefs, is the truth that you have come into the world for a mission, that you are here for a purpose and that God has sent you into the world to serve the world, under the very circumstances that are approaching you now.

In the face of the Great Waves of change, there is nowhere to run and hide.

Therefore, while in your mind you may respond with great

fear or trepidation, with anger and indignation—you may be immensely confused and perplexed; you may feel helpless and impotent in the face of such great challenges—but deeper within you, at the level of Knowledge, this indeed is your time. This is the time when the great calling will sound for you. This is the time when your greater gifts will come forward, for you yourself cannot bring them forward. They must be called out of you. And the calling must come from the world, for you cannot call yourself if the calling is to be genuine. You cannot initiate yourself into a greater life. For the calling must come from beyond you—calling your gifts out of you, calling you into a greater state of mind and awareness and into a greater position of responsibility.

Without this calling, you will simply either go into denial and try to forget and remain ignorant and foolish, or you will fight and struggle to preserve whatever entitlements you feel you have or that are still due to you. You will act out of fear and anger. You will lash out at others. You will be immensely afraid and incredibly confused. You will believe that something will save you, that there is a solution on the horizon that will make all these problems go away. You will not see and you will not know and you will not prepare. And when the Great Waves come, you will be unprepared, and you will be vulnerable.

This is the time when the great calling will sound for you. This is the time when your greater gifts will come forward.

Surely, you have seen that nature is unmerciful to the unprepared. Nature shows no mercy to those who are not prepared for eventualities. God wishes to save you failure, conflict and discord. That is why Knowledge has been placed within you. God knows what is coming for humanity. But people remain blind and foolish and self-indulgent. God knows that if you do not prepare, if you do not become strong with Knowledge, if you do not allow your gifts to be called out of you, if you cling to an old life, an old set of ideas and assumptions, then you will fail. And your failure will be terrible.

Yet Knowledge within you is ready to respond. It is not afraid of the Great Waves. In fact, it has been prepared for them all along, for this is your destiny. You did not come into the world simply to be a consumer, simply to occupy space, simply to further degrade the world and to use up its resources. That is not what has brought you here, and in your heart you know this to be true. But what you know to be true and what you think are not yet the same. And you must then align yourself with Knowledge and learn The Way of Knowledge and take the steps to Knowledge so that it becomes your guide and counsel.

You will need this inner certainty, for around you there will be confusion, anger and conflict as people are deprived, as people feel threatened, as the security of people everywhere becomes challenged. You will see individuals and groups reacting with rage and indignation. You will see nations threatening one another, and this is already happening. And the great conflicts that will emerge and the great danger of war will all be masked by politics and religion, when in fact the conflict is over resources. Who will have these resources? Who will control these resources?

Such conflicts have already begun and are well under way. And the prospect for greater conflicts, for greater wars, is growing with each passing day. There is already fire burning in the world, and the embers for greater fires of conflict are being stoked, and the conditions are ripe for their emergence.

Surely, if you want to be protected and to benefit from the great change that is coming, you cannot remain in your current position, your current way of thinking, your current assumptions. There must be a profound shift within you, and this shift will be brought about both by the conditions of the world and by the emergence of Knowledge within you. You cannot stay where you are mentally, psychologically and emotionally and have any real hope of surviving and benefiting from the great change that is coming.

This is the great warning that the New Message* is presenting. The Great Waves of change are coming to the world, and humanity is now facing competition from beyond the world— intervention from races beyond the world who seek to take advantage of a weak and divided humanity, who seek to benefit from the decline of human civilization. The New Message Teaching presents this reality very clearly. And it is not difficult to understand once you let down your defenses, once you set aside your preferences, once you look with clear eyes and listen to the world to see and to know.

The signs in the world are speaking to you—telling you that great change is coming, that it is at your doorstep.

Yet, remarkably, such common sense is not common. People are lost in what they want or in what they are afraid to lose. They are lost in their conflicts, in their grievances, in their struggles with themselves and each other. So what is clear and natural to see, to hear, to know and to do becomes lost— overlaid by human preoccupation, human desire and human conflict.

Surely, humanity is reaching a great threshold now that will determine its fate and its future. The evidence of this is all around you, and you can feel it within yourself—the sense of anxiety, the sense of uncertainty, the confusion, the apprehension. The signs in the world are speaking to you—telling you that great change is coming, that it is at your doorstep.

You can feel these things if you allow yourself to feel these

---

*See "Important Terms"

things—without trying to hide or run away from them, or without insisting that you be happy and carefree, without foolish pursuits to keep your mind preoccupied and distracted so that you do not hear the signs of the world, the calling of the world and the stirring of Knowledge within yourself.

This is your time. This is why you have come. These are the great events of your time. This is the great threshold that humanity is facing, for you must now prepare for a future that will be unlike the past. Life will not go on as you have known it, uninterrupted. Humanity will not simply find other sources of energy or some magic solution to maintain the privileges of the few.

For you are living in a world in decline. The very resources that give your nations wealth, security and stability are now diminishing. The environment in which you live will come under increasing duress through environmental degradation, through change in climate and through so many impacts that humanity has had for so long upon the world itself.

Therefore, you stand at the precipice. Will you choose to remain ignorant and will you fight and struggle when your ignorance and your denial fail you finally? Or will you choose the path of courage and wisdom to prepare and to allow God's great gift of Knowledge to guide you and to direct you?

To know the meaning of God's great gift, you must see the gravity and the depth of the challenge facing humanity. You must feel the need within yourself, recognizing that you yourself do not have an answer and that even your nations and your experts and your scientists do not really have an answer. They have solutions for parts of the problem. They are working towards alerting and preparing humanity, but humanity is way behind now in preparing for the Great Waves of change. The hour is late, and you are unprepared.

You therefore must feel the real need within yourself to respond to the great gift that God is giving now—a gift unlike anything humanity has ever received before—for humanity is now facing a challenge and a crisis unlike anything it has ever faced before.

To see the solution, you must feel the need. You must recognize the need. You must face the Great Waves of change. You must begin to piece together the pieces and the signs to see the picture that it is showing you. This picture is clear and obvious, but it is not obvious to those who are not looking, who are not thinking, who are not making the fundamental associations that must be made if you are to see the picture clearly.

You may be the only person you know who is responding. Even if this is the case, you must respond.

Any courageous course of action to redirect your focus and your energy always must be based upon an inner and pressing need. Under quiescent circumstances, people rarely make any progress at all in any field of endeavor. The real progress must be driven by a deep and pressing need—the pressure both from your circumstances and from the needs of the world and also from Knowledge within you. Knowledge is urging you to become aware. It is urging you to prepare yourself psychologically, emotionally and practically for the great challenges that are coming now, for the great events of your life and for the great relationships that you are meant to have. Yet these relationships will only arise in meeting a greater challenge in life.

Do not worry that others are not responding. Do not concern yourself that humanity remains ignorant and indulgent and foolish in its conquests and its conflicts. For the calling is for you. You have to take responsibility for your life and for your reasons for being here. The calling is for you. You do not need a consensus with others to respond. In fact, you will not have such a consensus. You may be the only person you know who is responding. Even if this is the case, you must respond. You cannot wait for others to give you the reassurance that you should respond, for when everyone responds, there will be panic and discord. There will be tribulation and conflict. You do not want to wait until the moment when everyone responds, for that will be chaos.

You must prepare yourself and your life. You must fortify your relationships. You must educate the people you know that are close to you—those who can hear and those who can respond. You must set aside your goals and preferences to respond to the world. You must reevaluate where you live, how you live and who you are with in terms of who can travel with you, who can prepare with you and who cannot. You must reevaluate your work and its viability for the future. And you must do this without everyone around you encouraging you and agreeing with you, for this will be unlikely.

Your mind will not want to face the future. Your mind will want other things because the mind is weak and fallible. It is driven by fear and preference. But there is a greater mind within you, the mind of Knowledge. It is not distracted. It is not in conflict with itself. It is not subject to seduction by the world or by any other force, for it only responds to God. It is the only part of you that is completely pure and reliable, and it is the only part of you that is wise. It contains your greater purpose for coming into the world, and it represents your fundamental relationship with God, which has not been lost in the Separation.

Despite all the appearances of this world, despite all of the activities and indulgences and tragedies of this world, you remain connected to God. And God has sent you into the world to serve a world in great need. That is why you are who you are. That is why you have a unique nature. That is why you have certain strengths that must be used and certain weaknesses that must be recognized and managed properly. For you cannot be weak and ambivalent in the face of the Great Waves of change. They will call out of you your core strength, and you will need this core strength now. You cannot be fooling around in the face of such great and immense difficulties and challenges.

Indeed, the Great Waves are converging on the world. You cannot escape them. They are profound and will be long lasting. Do you have the clarity, the sobriety and the honesty to see them clearly, to brace yourself for them emotionally and psychologically and begin to build a foundation for yourself—a foundation created by Knowledge within you, a foundation of relationships, a foundation of activities and a foundation of wisdom? You build this foundation not only to be able to navigate these great challenges, but to be able to assist and to serve others.

> *Though this seems overwhelming, though this is not what you prefer, this in fact is what will redeem you.*

For you must know that the human need will grow far greater in the future. Everyone will become poorer, and many will be destitute. You must have the strength here not only to take care of yourself but to take care of others as well—to take care of the elderly, to take care of children. Certainly, you yourself will not take care of everyone, but it will be clear who amongst your neighbors or your relations are especially weak and vulnerable. You must be strong enough to take care of them as well.

Though this seems overwhelming, though this is not what you prefer, this in fact is what will redeem you, for this will call you out of your conflicts, your addictions, your low self-esteem, your regrets, your painful memories. This will force you to establish a real relationship with yourself, with others and with the world.

So do not look upon the Great Waves of change only as a tragedy or as a great danger, but as a calling, as a require-ment—a calling and a requirement that can restore and redeem you, that can call forth Knowledge within you and the great gifts that you have come to give, gifts that will be determined by the very circumstances that are emerging now.

The Great Waves of change will bring great clarity to your life, and they will show you both your weakness and your strength. They will shake you out of your dreams of fulfillment and tragedy. They will bring you to your senses, and they will bring you to Knowledge within you. Therefore, do not repudiate them. Do not deny them. Do not think that they are insignificant or that people will have a simple solution to them, for to do so is to deny yourself the calling and the power of your time and the redemption that it is meant to bring to you who were sent into the world for these very circumstances.

This will reunite you with your strength, and it will break your attachment to your weaknesses, for it is you who must be called forth now. This is not a problem for others to take care of, for everyone must take a part. And the more who can be called into their greater purpose here, the greater will be the chances for humanity, the greater will be the promise for humanity and the greater will be the likelihood that humanity will be able to survive the Great Waves of change and to set a new course and a new direction and a greater unity and cooperation in the process.

The Great Waves of change will bring great clarity to your life, and they will show you both your weakness and your strength.

Yet it depends upon you and the strength that you were born with, the strength which must now come to the fore in the Knowledge that God has placed within you, which alone knows the way forward.

For the great times are upon you. This is your time. This is your calling. This is where your real strength will be found. Real strength is never found when people are complacent and asleep. It is only found when people are responding and acting with true direction and intention.

With the New Message Teaching, humanity now has great hope. For the first time, spirituality is being presented at the level of Knowledge. It is a great calling. It is a great gift. It brings with it wisdom beyond what humanity has ever established. It calls people out of the shadows—out of conflict, out of controversy, out of addiction, out of tragedy—to respond to a world in need.

For the New Message speaks to the great need of the world—the Great Waves of change and the Greater Darkness of intervention that is in the world. It speaks to the greater purpose that has called everyone here. It speaks to the power of Knowledge and reveals how Knowledge can be discovered and experienced. It speaks to the level of relationships that people must reach if they are to find real union and power with one another. It speaks of humanity's future in the Greater Community of intelligent life in the Universe and the great threshold that humanity must pass through to find its greater destiny and fulfillment.

You are blessed, then, to receive this Message, to be alerted to the Great Waves of change and to the Greater Darkness that is in the world. For you have time to become aware, to brace yourself and to prepare your life and to receive the guidance that God is giving you through the Knowledge that you were born with, which is God's greatest endowment to you and to the world.

CHAPTER 2

The Great Waves and Your Life

PEOPLE WILL ASK, "What will these Great Waves look like? What can we expect? What are we really preparing for? Is it a difficult situation or is it a terrible situation?" The answer depends upon many things—upon human response and responsibility.

Certainly, the resources of the world will be diminished, and there will be great difficulty in securing them, particularly in poor countries and for poor people. And the risk of conflict and war over these diminishing resources will be very great. The risk will be very great.

How will people respond? Will humanity destroy itself as it struggles and fights over who will get the remaining resources, or will there be a greater union and cooperation? The answer is uncertain, but in either case you are moving into a time of great difficulty.

The climate of the world will change and become warmer in most places—diminishing food production, diminishing water supplies, creating great difficulties in certain regions of the world. The risk of the breakdown of society is extremely great under these circumstances, and the fact that most people are either unaware of this or are taking it far too lightly gives great concern.

Humanity has overspent its natural inheritance. It has overused the world, this place of magnificence and abundance. Humanity has not planned for the future. It has not restrained

You will have to live very differently, and only Knowledge within you can guide you specifically in this matter.

its behavior. It has wasted its great natural inheritance through greed and through conflict, through misuse and corruption, and now it will have to face the consequences. You will have to pay for the sins of the past, as your children will have to pay for the sins of the present. These sins are errors, fundamental errors, and in some cases tremendous errors.

Therefore, you cannot escape this. You cannot move somewhere else and be immune from the Great Waves of change. You will have to live very differently, and only Knowledge within you can guide you specifically in this matter. Beyond following the "Recommendations for Living in a Great Waves World" that are included in this book, it will be up to Knowledge within you, the strength of your relationships with others and the courage and objectivity you can bring to your circumstances that will determine the path that you must follow. For everything will be changing, and there will be great uncertainty.

Where you live, how you live and who you are with will all have tremendous bearing on what kind of circumstances you will have to face. And you will have to gain access to Knowledge—the deeper mind within you, the mind that God has created within you—to answer these questions. The answer will not necessarily be an explanation, but a series of steps— things you must do, step by step. For great change requires that you move incrementally step by step. The only exception to this is being in an extreme emergency, such as being in a house on fire or on a sinking ship. But beyond this, you must follow a series of actions which may not make any sense to you at all in the moment, a series of actions which others might consider to be foolish or irrational. You will have to follow these.

Ask yourself, "Where should I live?" Keep asking, and the

steps will begin to appear if there is any change you must make in this regard. You cannot ask only once. You must ask repeatedly. You must be with the question. You must live with the question and be open, really open, to what might be presented to you, particularly if you already sense that where you are is not permanent, or you have concern over its viability as a place to live in the future.

You must be very open, you see, because Knowledge will not just take you to the place that is the safest or the easiest. It will guide you to the place where your greater strengths can emerge, where your destiny can be fulfilled and where you will be able to meet the really important people in your life and engage in the really important activities in your life.

This is entirely beyond the scope of just being safe and secure. And this is one of the reasons that people do not understand the answer when the answer is given. They do not understand or trust their deeper inclinations because they are asking the question with a hidden motive to get what they want—to be enriched, to be protected, to keep what they have or to have more. But this is not the emphasis of Knowledge. Knowledge will protect you here, but it will protect you and save you for a greater purpose.

In a way, the Great Waves of change provide a very optimum environment for Knowledge to emerge because there is really no place that you will be safe. There will be no place that will really be secure, where you can enjoy the kinds of benefits you might have enjoyed in the past, where you will feel safe and immune from the difficulties that will be emerging all around you.

The survival of your personality is not the issue here. It is the fulfillment of your mission. For you have chosen to come into the world at a time when the Great Waves would be

> *Knowledge will protect you here, but it will protect you and save you for a greater purpose.*

striking the world. You have come at a time when humanity would have to deal with competition from the Greater Community, from invasive forces from the Universe around you. You have come at a time of great difficulty and uncertainty, a time of great discord and risk of war. Therefore, do not be in complaint. Do not deny or condemn the circumstances of the world when, in fact, they hold the greatest possibility for your redemption and for your fulfillment here.

Your great relationships will not come to you while you are hiding out somewhere pretending to be happy, safe and secure, surrounded by all your unnecessary possessions, involved in simple and innocuous and foolish activities. The great relationships will not come to you under these circumstances, only casual friendships, only people who share your hobbies or others who want to exploit you or share in whatever wealth you might have.

You are going to have to be prepared to take dramatic action, and you may have to act alone.

The great relationships will come in facing great change and difficulty because it is within this environment that the deeper and truer nature of people becomes evident. And people will have to choose a greater allegiance within themselves and a greater allegiance to others. This is where great relationships become recognized, cultivated and expressed. No more foolish and indulgent romances here. No more wasting your time trying to have endless pleasure with someone when, in fact, you have nowhere to go together and nothing really important to do together. No more wasting your life on chasing beauty, charm and wealth; having fantasies about yourself and other people; trying to look good, to be accepted and degrading yourself in every possible way to gain the attraction or the admiration of some person. There will be little time for such things now.

While these times are extremely dangerous and hazardous,

they provide the optimum environment for you to discover your greater strengths and with this, a set of greater relationships. This is where the greater purpose and meaning of your life can emerge if you can understand your situation correctly and if you learn to engage with your deeper nature and to rely upon it increasingly.

Here you must respond when others are not responding. You must take precautions when others are not taking precautions. You must change your circumstances when there appears to be no immediate reason for doing it. You must follow an inner urging and an inner direction, without really understanding what is happening and what your future or the outcome will look like. If you do not have the strength or courage to do this, you will just stand where you are, becoming increasingly full of anxiety and confusion, increasingly worried, increasingly frustrated and compulsive until your circumstances just fall away and erode your life, like a person who is standing on a slowly shrinking island or in a boat that is taking on water increasingly.

You are going to have to be prepared to take dramatic action, and you may have to act alone. Not everyone who is with you now—your friends or even your family—will necessarily respond to the Great Waves of change or to the power and influence of Knowledge within them. Just being worried and concerned is not enough. Just being aware of the problem is not enough. You must be prepared to act—not hastily, not compulsively, not in a panic, but carrying out steps in your preparation.

The New Message has provided *Steps to Knowledge* so that you can begin to build this deeper connection to Knowledge, a connection that you will have to rely upon increasingly in the future as all other sources of certainty become challenged, upset and in conflict.

For where will you turn, who will you turn to in times of great change and uncertainty? Your government? Your friends?

Your family? Your religion? And if you cannot find any certainty or clarity there, will you run away into your hobbies or your fantasies or your passions? This is a critical question, you see.

God has given you Knowledge to guide you, to protect you and to lead you to a greater fulfillment in the world as it is. Therefore, do not ask anything more from God. If you cannot receive this great endowment—a gift beyond your estimation, a gift that will serve you every day and in every circumstance—if you cannot receive *this*, if you will not trust *this*, if you will not follow *this*, then do not ask for a miracle. You may ask, but you are going to have to rely upon what God has given you. You have created a world where this will be increasingly necessary, a world where fantasy, speculation and presumption will be increasingly difficult to create and maintain.

Times will become more difficult. People will become more impoverished. Everything will become more expensive and in some cases unavailable. How will you function in this environment? You will have to turn to simple pleasures—the pleasure of the moment, the beauty of nature, connecting with other people in a significant way, enjoying very simple things. Relationships will have to be simple and honest now. Though many people will use deception to gain advantage over others, relationships will have to become very simple, direct and honest.

In a way, your life will have to become more authentic, more healthy and more in balance instead of this frantic pursuit to fulfill your fantasies and your needs, your expectations and the expectations of others—this frantic, desperate, unhappy life where you have no sense of yourself or where you are going or what you are really about.

So even in the face of the Great Waves of change, even in the face of the dangers of intervention and competition from beyond the world, you have an opportunity to bring your life into order, to establish a genuine set of priorities and to stop wasting your time, your energy and your life force on things that have no meaning, value or purpose. You have the opportunity to become strong, integrated, balanced, courageous, objective and compassionate, whereas before you were simply an addict of your culture, trying to have, be and do things that were not essential to your nature or to your greater purpose for being here.

Here your relationship with yourself becomes critical, fundamental, practical and mysterious. Whatever difficulties you have had from the past and whatever defects or deficiencies you now have will be overshadowed by the need of the moment and the need to prepare for the future. This is the perfect antidote to self-obsession and mental illness, to poor mental health and poor emotional

Relationships will have to be simple and honest now.

health. You will have to do things now you have never had to do, to learn things you have never had to learn, to become resourceful and observant.

Do not look at the future, thinking and worrying about what you might lose. Recognize that the future has the power to uplift you, to give you back to yourself, to restore to you your true purpose for coming here and your true capabilities. But you must gain access to Knowledge, for only Knowledge knows who you are, why you are here and how you will be able to navigate the difficult times ahead.

If you can prepare in advance, you will be in a position to help others. If you wait, the change you will have to make will be desperate, expensive and hazardous. If you put it off or question it or doubt it or think it is not important, you will put yourself in ever-increasing jeopardy, and your chances of success will diminish as a result.

This is not an idle matter. This is not mere speculation. The New Message is telling you what is coming. It is warning you. It is preparing you. But it is still up to you to respond, to be responsible—to be able to respond and to learn how to follow, step by step, the things that you must do, with courage and determination.

Time is important now. You do not have time to languish. You do not have time to be distracted, carried away with other things or caught up in the circumstances of your life. There is no time for this now. You must take your life seriously. You must pay attention to the signs of the world that are telling you that great change is coming. You must learn to listen to the movement of Knowledge and the urging of Knowledge within yourself.

Your study of *Steps to Knowledge* will teach you how to read the signs of the world and the signs of Knowledge, for this is a very different kind of education, unlike anything the world itself can provide. This education is without fantasy. It is without prejudice. It is without an idealistic view of the future. It is without human compromise and human corruption. It is pure and powerful, and you must become powerful to engage with it, and it will give you this power, indeed.

There will be great human need in the future. Many people will not have enough food or shelter. There will be great civil unrest in the large cities and in smaller communities as well. You must be strong enough not only to gain a secure position for yourself, but also to assist others, especially the elderly and the young. Lives will be lost through conflict and deprivation. This will depend upon whether nations and cultures choose to share the resources of the world or to try to gain them for themselves.

So there is a range of outcomes here from difficult to terrible. It is not up to you to determine the outcome. It is up to you to prepare for the future and to live fully in the moment— eyes wide open, paying attention, being responsible and exerting yourself appropriately. You do not need to read many books now. You do not need to go see movies. You do not need to engage in endless and pointless conversations with people. You do not need to immerse yourself in your hobbies and your interests. Only what is essential and deeply meaningful to you should you focus on.

You have Four Pillars in your life. Like the four legs of a table, they uphold your life. Think of your life then in terms of having Four Pillars—a Pillar of Relationships, a Pillar of Health, a Pillar of Work and Providership and a Pillar of Spiritual Development. Your life is only as strong as the weakest Pillar, the weakest leg of the table. How much you can see, how much you can know and how much you can do will be dependent upon the strength of these Pillars.

Most people's Pillars are barely built. Perhaps they have put all their emphasis in one area. They have focused their whole life on relationships, or they have focused their entire life on their work and their career, or they have become obsessed with their health, and it dominates everything that they do. Or perhaps they have run away and tried to immerse themselves in their spiritual practice and religious beliefs, while allowing the rest of their lives to be undeveloped and out of balance.

You have Four Pillars in your life. Like the four legs of a table, they uphold your life.

There are few people who have built two Pillars. But very few people have adequately built all Four Pillars of their lives. To do so is a perfect antidote to eccentricity and extremism. For if you are really building and maintaining the Four Pillars of your life, you cannot be extreme or eccentric in any area. You cannot be compulsive. You cannot be addicted because you will be so busy taking care of the fundamental Pillars of your life, you will not have time for foolishness or self-destructive behaviors. What a blessing this would be, and the results are profound, giving you a strong life, a broad set of abilities and competence in every aspect of your life.

Your Pillar of Relationships must include people who are capable of responding to the Great Waves of change—people who function not from fear and anxiety, but from certainty and conviction and the desire to support and assist the world.

Your Pillar of Work must represent work that is sustainable into the future—work that provides real goods or services to people, work that engages you meaningfully with others and that can provide at least the basics of what you need to live in the world.

The stronger your foundation, the better equipped you will be to weather the storms of the world.

In your Pillar of Health, your body and your mind must function as vehicles for Knowledge. For the body serves the mind, and the mind serves the Spirit in the true hierarchy of your Being. You do not have to be beautiful or athletic or fantastic in any regard, just functional. Good health, good mental health, good emotional health, self-honesty, honesty with others, the ability to appreciate and enjoy the moment, the ability to recognize and prepare for the future, the ability to connect with Knowledge and have a real foundation in your life and the ability to have simple and rewarding enjoyments and artistic expression—these represent the Pillar of Health.

The Pillar of Spiritual Development fundamentally is about your connection to Knowledge—building this connection, relying upon this connection, learning the wisdom to carry it out into the world, learning how to apply it and recognize it and discerning the power of Knowledge from all other compulsions or influences in your mind. Whatever your spiritual practice might be, whatever religious faith you might have, or even if you do not have a religious faith that you can define, it is your connection to Knowledge that connects you to what God has given you to protect you, to guide you and to lead you to a greater fulfillment and service to the world. This is your Pillar of Spiritual Development.

You need to build these Four Pillars. It is essential for the future, for times will become difficult and unstable. The stronger your foundation, the better equipped you will be to weather the storms of the world and to deal with the increasing chaos as people's confusion, anguish and rage increase all around you. You will need to know where to go, what to do, what to say, what not to say, where to give yourself, where not to give yourself, what to involve yourself in, what not to involve yourself in, where to speak out, where not to speak out, where to travel and where not to travel.

You must have this foundation; otherwise, the Great Waves will wash you away. You will feel overwhelmed. Your life will be overtaken, and you will be left destitute and subject to very dark influences in the world and even from beyond the world. Again, the difficulty of the times is the perfect opportunity for you to reconnect with your life, to build your Four Pillars, to reestablish your integrity, to take determined action and to learn to be courageous and objective.

It is not about perception here, whether you are loving or fearful. It is really about whether you are wise or unwise, whether you are responsible or irresponsible. Do not hold yourself apart and think it is all about perception. The Great Waves are far more powerful than you are. You will not alter them with your affirmations or your declarations. But you can learn to mitigate them, to adapt to them, to use them to your advantage and to use them to be of assistance to others.

The human need around you will be immense—greater than any world war it will be. And you will have to be prepared to take care of people, people you do not even know perhaps, and to assist others in ways that will be new for you and unexpected. There will be great shortages of food and in some places great shortages of water. Your energy resources will become precious,

It is not about perception here, whether you are loving or fearful. It is really about whether you are wise or unwise, whether you are responsible or irresponsible.

difficult and expensive to gain access to. There will be political and economic instability, and there will be much civil unrest in many places in the world.

This is humanity's greatest hour, greatest challenge, greatest danger and greatest opportunity for unity and cooperation.

This is the world you have come to serve, and the more you are connected to Knowledge within yourself, the more you will gain this recognition, which will quiet your fears and your anxiety and affirm your strength and your great Source and all of the meaningful relationships that are here to serve and to assist you.

You have come to serve a world in transition, a world that will have to unite in many ways to meet the fundamental needs of the human family, a world that will have to prepare itself to deal with difficult interventions from races from beyond the world who are here to take advantage of a weak and divided humanity.

This is humanity's greatest hour, greatest challenge, greatest danger and greatest opportunity for unity and cooperation, where the resources of humanity and the great talents of humanity come together to sustain civilization, to restore the world and to prepare for your future and your destiny within a Greater Community of intelligent life in the Universe.

Yet you will have to take a very different tack with it, a different approach. You will have to learn how to do this and gain strength, and quickly, for time is of the essence now. Each month and each year is critical in determining whether you are becoming stronger or weaker, more prepared or less prepared, more certain or less certain, more connected to others in a meaningful way or less connected.

The awareness of the Great Waves of change is God's great calling for you and great gift to you who are fortunate enough to read these words. For it is a great love that brings this warning, this blessing and this preparation into the world—a love for humanity, a love for the possibilities for humanity and a concern to provide for humanity what it will need to see, know and do to prepare to live in a radically changing world and to prepare for your future within the Greater Community, which represent your greater destiny now.

Receive this awareness as a gift of great love, for great love it is. Receive it as a confirmation of what you most deeply know, for a confirmation it is. Accept it as a gift out of love and respect, for such it is. Use it and follow it to the best of your ability, for that is how you honor your relationship with God. And that is how you will fulfill the great purpose that has brought you here at this time.

CHAPTER 3

Escaping the Past

HUMANITY IS PREPARING to live in a very different future, a future unlike the past in so many ways. The accelerating change that you experience around yourself and even within yourself gives testimony to this. But it is not merely that your immediate circumstances are going through change or that you are perhaps having new kinds of experiences within yourself. The whole world is changing. For the Great Waves of change are upon the world, and humanity is now facing Contact and intervention from intelligent races in the Universe, from the Greater Community of life in which your world exists.

To be able to recognize this and to respond to it accordingly, you have to be able to think clearly. You have to be able to see clearly, with great objectivity. You have to bring common sense to your decisions. But this seems remarkably difficult for people and has always been difficult for people because their thoughts reflect the past. Their assumptions reflect the past. They assume and believe that the future will be like the past.

This has become so ingrained that people even think that life is a set of cycles like the past—economic cycles, life cycles— as if the past is simply reasserting itself, recreating itself over and over again like the perpetual continuance of the seasons, or the rising and falling of the sun. This past orientation prevents people from seeing clearly, prevents them from bringing common sense to a new set of questions, prevents them from

If you do not see these things and respond appropriately, change will have a devastating impact upon you. It will overtake you. You did not see it coming.

recognizing that their lives are changing and that they have to make decisions now that are perhaps unlike anything they have ever had to do before.

Many people want to escape the past because of their failures and their disappointments. These things can haunt them and often do. But escaping the past has a far greater importance here. Its importance is related to your ability to see and know the truth in the moment and to respond to the changing circumstances of your life.

If you do not see these things and respond appropriately, change will have a devastating impact upon you. It will overtake you. You did not see it coming. You did not recognize the consequences. You did not see the importance of making a decision way back when you had the opportunity to make the decision. So much regarding success and failure in life depends on the ability to see, to know and to respond appropriately, even facing decisions you are unaccustomed to, even facing circumstances you are not adapted to and are not used to.

God has put within you a greater intelligence to help you make these decisions, to help you to see and recognize a set of circumstances that you must respond to. God has given you the eyes to see and the ears to hear. But because the mind is so fixated in the past and on the assumptions from the past, this seeing and this hearing are greatly impeded and in many cases overwhelmed.

The past you are escaping is not merely your own sense of failure, loss and disappointment from previous times. It is really the influence of the past on your ability to look ahead, to see what is coming over the horizon of your life, to recognize the Great Waves of change in a timely manner so that you may be able to respond to them, prepare yourself for them and so that you may have the time to change the circumstances or the situations in your life appropriately.

Knowledge within you will warn you far in advance of danger and difficulty. But if you cannot hear what Knowledge is telling you or if you do not take its messages seriously—dismissing them as mere obscurities or fears that must be overcome—then you will not benefit from the great voice that God has placed within you. And though you are intelligent, you will not function in an intelligent manner. For real intelligence is the ability and the desire to learn and to adapt. This is what real intelligence is. Real intelligence is not simply solving complex problems or building complex machines or being clever and witty. For if you cannot see and you cannot know, what advantage do these aspects of your mind give you? If you cannot respond intelligently to life, then what is the value of your intelligence?

God knows what is coming over the horizon, and that is why there is a New Message in the world. But if you cannot see it, if you cannot respond to it, if you cannot mount the effort to do those things that it is telling you to do, then this New Message will seem to be lost upon you, and the great endowment of Knowledge that has been given you will not be yours to benefit from.

Many people speak of possibilities regarding the future. The future could be this; the future could be that. This may happen; that may happen. The Earth may get warmer; the Earth may get colder. There is endless speculation, but no vision, no Knowledge and no recognition. People can spend a great deal of time in speculation and in debate over the possibilities for this or the possibilities for that. But the speculation is all based upon the past—past assumptions, past

Real intelligence is the ability and the desire to learn and to adapt.

People base their whole lives on a set of unquestioned assumptions about the continuance of things that they recognize and are accustomed to.

orientation, past beliefs, past experiences, the history of their lives and the history of humanity. But if there is no recognition, if there is no real insight, then all of this time and energy and debate and speculation are for nothing. It has not benefited you at all.

In debate, you will rest upon the assumptions that you are most accustomed to. You will seek to reinforce what you already believe to be true. You will try to defend your position, assert your perspective and solidify your beliefs to reinforce the past. This tremendously wasteful expenditure of your energy, time and resources is actually just an attempt to reassert what you already think is true and to overcome any objections to this. Self-fulfilling this is and self-defeating all at once.

The truth in life is that you do not know what is going to happen next unless Knowledge gives you an insight or a clue. People base their whole lives on a set of unquestioned assumptions about the continuance of things that they recognize and are accustomed to. But life can give you a new experience and can rob you of your abilities in a moment. Things can change for you dramatically in a moment—a great accident, a great loss, a great illness, a tragic set of events in your community, war, pestilence, drought, famine or flooding. The list goes on and on, and yet people are not wary. They are not looking. They are not paying attention. They are not reading the signs of the world that are telling them that great change is upon them.

Before there is a great illness, there are signs. Before there is a great drought, there are signs. Before there is a failure in your activities, there are signs. Before a relationship fails, there are signs. Before any great mistake, there are signs. Yet who is paying attention? Who is looking? Who has the clarity of mind to see these signs and to interpret them in the moment for what they really are and for what they really reveal?

If you are not reading the signs of the world, you are not behaving in an intelligent manner. You are not using your intelligence, the greater intelligence that God has given you—not your social conditioning, not your appeasement of other people's expectations of you, not your constant striving to gain material success or to win approval from others, but the great intelligence that the Creator of all life has given you to see, to know and to act with commitment and certainty.

Before any great mistake, there are signs. Yet who is paying attention?

The signs are there. Great Waves are coming to the world, converging upon humanity—environmental degradation, changing climate, the loss of resources, the depletion of the world, the decline of the world and the presence of an intervention from beyond the world by races who are here to take advantage of a weak and divided humanity.

There are so many signs. The world is telling you what is coming. It is warning you. It is trying to get your attention. But your attention is always on other things—on your internal problems, on your internal conflicts, on your memories, on your hopes, on your dreams, on your fears, on your constant activities and constant stimulation.

Humanity has at this time reached a great threshold, a turning point where change on a scale that has never occurred in the world before is beginning now to take place. You cannot avoid this. You cannot run away and hide somewhere, pack your bags and move to the country, or move to another country. Wherever you go, wherever you are, the Great Waves

The world is telling you what is coming. It is warning you. It is trying to get your attention.

While your mind, your intellect, does not know what will happen next, Knowledge within you is responding to the signs from the world.

will be there, and the impacts will grow over time and in many places will be catastrophic.

The world is telling you this. Knowledge within yourself is telling you this because it is the truth. It is not dependent upon a person's perspective, attitude or beliefs. These do not change the great circumstances that are coming. Whether you are loving or fearful will only either help you or disable you from recognizing the truth of your situation. It is not a matter of perspective. Do not fool yourself in thinking this. Do not try to bypass the power of recognition that God has placed within you that will protect you and guide you and ultimately place you in a position to be of great service to others.

While your mind, your intellect, does not know what will happen next, Knowledge within you is responding to the signs from the world and from the wisdom from God. Therefore, fundamental to your preparation is building a relationship with Knowledge, taking the steps to Knowledge and gaining access to the wisdom and the power that God has placed within you, which now, more than ever before, will be essential for your survival and success.

To project into the future expectations based upon the past is really only a form of dreaming and fantasizing. It is not intelligent. To think you are going to have more than your parents had, to think that the world is going to give you whatever you want, to think that life will yield to your preferences and to your objectives is to be foolish and self-defeating.

Now at this great threshold, you will have to read the signs very carefully and very objectively, both from what the world is telling you and from what Knowledge within you is indicating, in order to begin to navigate a changing set of circumstances, a changing set of situations—navigating the troubled waters ahead.

Here you must stop dreaming, stop speculating and stop fantasizing in order to take the time to become still, to listen, to look and to allow the realization to slowly come together for you. Here there are no quick answers and immediate solutions. People want these things and expect them because they do not have the strength to face uncertainty. They do not have the skill and the maturity to face a set of circumstances that they cannot at first understand. So they want or demand solutions, answers, things that are simple, things that do not require any work from them or any participation from them, for they want to keep on dreaming, keeping their life of fantasy going so the world does not impinge upon them or demand anything from them.

If you understand what real intelligence is, you will see how remarkably foolish this is and how it will lead people to their own demise. You will see how it prevents one from receiving the wisdom and the grace of God. For God is not going to come and change all the circumstances to give you what you want. What you want is what is fooling you, what is obsessing you and what is dominating your attention—getting what you want, having what you want, dreaming about what you want, trying to manipulate yourself and other people to get what you want. Beyond meeting the basic necessities of life, this pursuit becomes ever more self-deceiving. It robs you of intelligence, wisdom and ability.

The past here will always pull you back, pull you back into a life of fantasy and speculation, argument and debate, a life where you only want to look at certain things and not at others, a life

Here there are no quick answers and immediate solutions. People want these things and expect them because they do not have the strength to face uncertainty.

where you do not want to recognize the truth of your situation or see the evidence of great change coming over the horizon.

This is tragic. It is tragic not only because of the outcome, but it is tragic because of the loss of your ability to gain the great wisdom and power that God has given you and its service to the world through you. Here not only does your life succumb to the Great Waves of change, but you are denied the possibility of providing a great contribution to life.

Here dreams of success and fulfillment, happiness and contentment, have taken you away from being really engaged in life—an engagement that will bring you true satisfaction, true ability and the possibility of fulfilling your greater purpose for coming into the world. You have given away something great for something very small and insignificant. You have chosen a little pleasure and have forfeited a great satisfaction.

God is not going to come and fix everything up for everyone, but God has placed Knowledge within everyone. Only Knowledge can lead you to act courageously, to act wisely and to act in such a way that you are able to benefit from a changing set of circumstances and to be of service to others, which will provide great satisfaction to you.

Look at history and it will teach you these lessons. In that respect, the past is a great teacher. Look at people living at the dawn of times of great change, at the outset of times of great change, and see the consequences for those who were aware and made preparations and the consequences for those who did not. Here history can be a great teacher, a great teacher of wisdom.

You are now living at the threshold of great change in the world. If you do not respond to this and cannot fulfill what Knowledge has given you to do, then these times will be terrifying and unsettling, and you will not be in a position to escape the difficulties, to benefit from the opportunities or to be of service to others.

This is why you must become serious about your life. You must look to your life. Stop playing games. Stop fantasizing and become engaged in life. Pay attention to what the world is telling you, but do not come to immediate conclusions. Do not look for simple answers. Do not demand solutions. For the Great Waves of change that are coming to the world and humanity's emergence into the Greater Community are problems you will have to live with. They are long-term situations that you will have to learn to deal with step by step. You will have to live with them and let the solutions come to you and to others gradually, for no one has an answer for these things. No one has a solution to the Great Waves of change. There are many people who see solutions to aspects of the Great Waves, but no one has an answer or a solution to the whole thing.

Pay attention to what the world is telling you, but do not come to immediate conclusions.

No one has an answer to how to prepare for the Greater Community, for how could they know—unaware of what life is like beyond the boundaries of this world, unaware of the complexities of engagement between nations in the Universe in your own vicinity and unaware of what governs life and commerce in this region of space that you will have to become educated about? Only a New Revelation can give you insight here. But even here, you have to grow and advance, for real learning is a step-by-step process. It does not happen all at once. Only those who are lazy, indolent and weak think they are gaining a great understanding in the moment. That is never the case. You learn in stages because you grow in stages. Great problems and challenges cannot be resolved quickly.

This is what life has always taught, and it is this that you must learn now if you are to gain real strength and ability in the face of the Great Waves of change. You will have to take steps, not always certain if they are the right steps, not always certain of the results that they will produce and not in control of the process. You will have to become stronger, more observant and more careful in what you do, in what you say and in what you give yourself to. But this is the price of wisdom. This is the price of having strength and ability, for you cannot be fooling around in the face of the Great Waves of change.

Take the lessons from history, but look ahead. Clear your mind. Set aside your assumptions. Set aside your beliefs and your preferences so that you may see, so that you may know, so that you may respond to the signs of the world and to the signs of Knowledge within you.

At first, these signs will seem subtle and perhaps indistinct, but over time they will become extremely clear and powerful. You will marvel at how you ever could have ignored them or overlooked them before. This will give you strength and confidence that Knowledge will speak to you in the future, and if you are in a position to follow it with strength and commitment, without assumptions, you will be able to navigate what to others will seem incomprehensible and overwhelming.

You cannot be fooling around in the face of the Great Waves of change.

You will be able to see the gift where others only see the loss. You will be able to recognize what you yourself must do and become, while others fall away and are overtaken.

You will see, with greater and greater clarity as you proceed, how the past has fooled you, how the past has diluted your awareness, how the past has kept you vague and self-obsessed and how the past has kept you locked in an experience of yourself as being weak and incompetent. You will have to have humility here, for the situation will be bigger than you are, and you will not have easy answers to rely upon.

It is because these are the Great Waves of change—immense they are, and long standing. They are the product of humanity's misuse of the world, the product of humanity's greed, humanity's conflicts, humanity's overuse of the resources of the world and humanity's ignorance about life in the Greater Community.

Life is moving, and you must move with it.

There is no escaping the consequences, for life is moving, and you must move with it. Circumstances will be changing in an increasing manner. You must be able to see what this will tell you to do and to become stronger with Knowledge so that you can discern the right moment to act and the right action to take.

Around you there will be increasing discord, anger, frustration, chaos and confusion. People will be upset. People will be enraged. People will be living in anxiety. People will be having great difficulty. Here you can only look to other individuals who are responding with Knowledge and to Knowledge within yourself, for around you everyone else will be panicking or will be trying to fool themselves increasingly in the face of great change.

The mental environment will become ever more discordant. People will be snapping out of their dreams of self-fulfillment with great difficulty and tremendous fear. People will be behaving in a self-destructive manner. Foolishness, confusion, hostility and conflict will grow around you. How will you be able to maintain your focus, your clarity, your self-awareness and your connection to Knowledge in this increasingly difficult environment? This is an important question. And it can only be answered by building a foundation in Knowledge, by learning about the Great Waves of change and by considering everything that you do and whether these things will be able to be sustained into the future.

Knowledge will lead you to act when action must be taken even if no one else is taking that action.

You will have to change when others are not changing. You will have to go right when everyone else is going left. You will have to respond when no one seems to respond or to even care. Knowledge will lead you to act when action must be taken even if no one else is taking that action.

Here you cannot rely upon consensus or the agreement of those people whose approval you think you must have. You have to become tremendously sober, self-reliant and clear minded. You have to gain control over your emotions and your reactions sufficiently so that you can maintain an awareness of where you are and who you are, no matter what is going on around you. And you will have to overcome the temptations of fear to go into denial, avoidance or blaming others.

This will not be easy, but it is redemptive, for this is where your great strength comes forward. This is where the power of Knowledge begins to reveal its true reality and significance in your life. Here is where your real gifts to the world have an opportunity to emerge where they could never emerge before. Here you will be living not a life of comfort and preference, but a life of clarity and meaningful engagement with others and with the world. For the comforts will fall away. The indulgences will become impossible. And yet it will be a time of great compassion, a time of great giving, a time where great relationships will be initiated and will grow and a time of redemption in the face of immense and seemingly overwhelming difficulties.

For this, you will need to take a different position with yourself—not as a slave to your wishes and your fears, not as a weak, pathetic person, but as someone who was sent into the world to serve the world under the very circumstances that will be growing around you. What happened before in your life will seem ever more remote as

> *What happened before in your life will seem ever more remote as you respond directly to what life is putting in your path today and tomorrow and and in all the days to follow.*

you respond directly to what life is putting in your path today and tomorrow and in all the days to follow. What you thought you were, what you thought you wanted, your preoccupations, your great conflicts with yourself and your past disappointments and failures, will all become further and further lost in the past, washed downstream in the river of life. For when you are living fully in the moment and preparing for the future, the past

You will have compassion for others, for you will see how difficult it really is to change your relationship with yourself and your relationship with the world.

cannot haunt you. It cannot overwhelm you, for your life is given to things that are more immediate and are more significant.

You escape the past by engaging in the present and by preparing for the future. Some aspects of your past will continue to serve you, and some aspects of your past will continue to bother you, but overall your emphasis will be on living in the moment and preparing for the future.

This engagement with life is life giving and is life restoring. Here Knowledge becomes more significant than your memories. Here the experience of clarity becomes more important than the seeming significance of your ideas or beliefs. Here your ability to see and to respond becomes ever more important for your well-being than your cherished ideas from the past. Here you are willing to sacrifice who you thought you were to allow yourself to become, over time, a greater person serving a greater purpose. Here your friends will change, your acquaintances will change, your priorities will change, your actions will change, your awareness will change—all to move you into a greater and more secure position in life.

Here you must have great compassion for others, for there will be tremendous failure and confusion all around you. Yet if you can undertake this preparation yourself, which is your destiny to do, you will have compassion for others, for you will see how difficult it really is to change your relationship with yourself and your relationship with the world. You will see how much of a focused effort this requires on your part—a sustained effort over time and through many situations. You will understand the challenge. You will see that everything in life that is meaningful is the product of commitment and consistent self-application. You will see its value for you and for others. And you will become a source of strength when others' strength seems to fail.

CHAPTER 4

The Freedom to Move with Knowledge

THERE ARE GROWING NUMBERS OF PEOPLE in the world today who sense that great change is coming, and more than this they have begun to respond to messages from Knowledge, the deeper intelligence within them telling them to do certain things, to make certain adjustments or changes in their lives and to take certain forms of action.

Yet so many of these people have been unable to respond. They feel the warning of the message or perhaps they see the signs, but they are not moved to act. They recognize the need. They recognize a possible danger. But they have not responded. They have not taken any action regarding it.

This represents two problems. The first is that Knowledge is not yet strong enough within the individual to move them. Knowledge is actually strong enough, but they do not have a strong enough connection to it to feel the urgency and the movement within themselves. It is like a distant voice or a passing image or a fleeting emotion, as if Knowledge were communicating to them, but from far away, through a great, thick wall. Knowledge is powerful within them, but they are not yet able to respond to it.

So this inability to respond, or this ir-response-ability you could say, is a fundamental problem. That is why in the study of *Steps to Knowledge*, there is a process of building a bridge from your thinking mind—from your intellect—which has been so formulated through social conditioning and past experience, to the deeper mind of Knowledge that God has created, that is beyond the reach of social conditioning, that cannot be manipulated or altered by any worldly or other-worldly force.

Building this bridge is very important because many people will see the signs, feel the signs within themselves, see the signs within the world, but they will not respond. They may shake their heads and say, "Oh, well, this is concerning." They may tell their friends, "Oh, I had a thought today that was worrying me," or "I see something happening in the world, and it could be very difficult." They are responding, but not at the level of action. These signs are arousing concern. They are arousing suspicion. They are alerting the individual, but the individual cannot yet really respond.

So while these signs are being recognized, the person just continues doing what they always do, carrying on their daily life as if nothing has happened. Yes, there is a growing concern. Yes, they sense that great change and difficulty are approaching. Yes, they may be aware of certain specific areas where difficulties are already arising. But they are not responding in a way that will move their lives.

Signs are not given to you just for your edification, just for your entertainment, just to arouse alarm or concern. They are given to instruct you and in many cases to move you to certain kinds of action. But you must feel these messages. They cannot be distant little images or fleeting emotions or passing thoughts. You must engage with them more powerfully in order to receive the instruction that they contain.

The world itself will tell you what is coming if you know how to read it and to discern its signs and its messages. You do this without projecting any of your own thoughts or fantasies or fears. You just watch and you listen, and piece by piece, the picture comes together. But to have this clarity of mind, you must be watching without coming to conclusions, without trying to tie things together, without trying to make things simple and comprehensible. Instead, like building a puzzle, you allow the pieces to emerge and to fit together.

This is called *seeing*. Most people do not see because they do not look with this emphasis. Impatient, they want conclusions. They want solutions. They want answers. They want to understand it right now. They want the picture to be evident right now—evident and comprehensible. They do not patiently wait and watch for the signs to tell them, allowing the picture to become clear, without their interference. This is called seeing.

It is the same with hearing. You hear certain things, but instead of drawing conclusions or having these things reinforce your current assumptions and beliefs, you let them simply reside in your mind— building. Let them instruct you instead of trying to use them to fortify your own ideas or position.

For all of humanity now there is growing danger, and nature has equipped you to respond to it.

All this requires humility, of course, and the willingness and the commitment to set aside assumptions, prejudices, preconceived ideas and so forth. To see and to hear truly, you must have this approach. But you must look earnestly, and you must listen earnestly. You must commit yourself to seeing and to hearing. It is not a casual pursuit you do once in a while. It is not something you do periodically, just to have a look or have a listen. It is what the animals do. They are always looking and listening, for there is danger, and they are equipped to respond to it, or they could not survive.

For all of humanity now there is growing danger, and nature has equipped you to respond to it, and you need to respond to it in order to survive. Yet people are not looking and are not listening. They go about their affairs without looking over the horizon, without listening to the signs of the world. And if they hear something, they will dismiss it, or discuss it with their friends, or use it to reinforce some attitude or judgment they have against someone else, and the message will be lost on them. They will not be able to receive the instruction, which will give them an indication of something they must do.

If people see and hear, but do not take action, then they have not really seen. They have not really heard. It has not passed beyond the intellect to reach deeper within them. They are not really responding, and so they are not really being responsible.

To prepare for the Great Waves of change, you will have to take many actions. Some of them will seem very illogical in the moment. You will not be able to justify them or explain them to others. But you must take them anyway because Knowledge within you, the deeper intelligence within you, is urging you. You can respond to this if your connection to Knowledge is becoming stronger. Now it is no longer a still small voice or a fleeting image or a moment of recognition. It is now something that is emerging within you as a deeper conviction, as an abiding concern or need. No longer can you ignore it, deny it or push it away so easily, for it is now competing for your attention.

To begin, you must learn to become still and observant— looking without judging, looking without coming to conclusions, looking for signs. The signs are not everywhere, but they are abundant enough that if you are observant and give yourself to being observant as you pass through your day, then you will begin to see things, and they will stand out from everything else. They will stand out. They will impress you more than just the usual kinds of fascinating things or disturbing things you may hear about or read about. They will impress you at a deeper level. Pay attention. Write them down. Keep a record of them with a date and a time and a place so you can begin to bring the pieces of the puzzle together.

You should be looking more and thinking less, listening more and speaking less, observing others without condemnation or judgment, setting aside your habits of judgment and evaluation in order to listen. Remember, the birds in the air and the animals in the field are always listening and watching. They must pay attention.

Humanity, which for so long has been involved in its great indulgences, its great conflicts, its great obsessions and addictions must now listen and look and pay attention without trying to falsely fortify itself and without trying to cast gloom and fear over everything. Now it is time to listen, to pay attention. It is a strange thing that the creature who is the most intelligent in the world, the human being, is functioning and acting in the least intelligent way.

The inner preparation is more important than the outer preparation.

Therefore, God must give a great warning. And the warning must be given with compassion, but with clarity and strength because people are in the habit of not looking and not listening and not paying attention. They do not know how to discern the signs of the world or the signs from Knowledge within themselves. And they are not close enough to Knowledge within themselves to feel the movement of Knowledge within them—Knowledge moving them to do something, to take action or to alter their activities in some specific way.

People think that to prepare for difficulties, you just fortify yourself from the outside. You stock up your house with food, or you just try to take a more defensive position. Or in extreme cases, you act as if you were on the verge of war, and you remove yourself to some distant location far away in the country, you arm yourself, and you look at everything fearfully.

But this is foolishness, for the inner preparation is more important than the outer preparation. For you do not know what you are preparing for yet. You cannot tell how things will go. And because you are ultimately here to serve humanity rather than to run away from humanity, you are really not engaging with the truth about your life if you simply try to build security for yourself. And any security you build for yourself will still be insecure in the face of the Great Waves of change.

You cannot run away and hide under a rock. You are going to need others to help you. You are going to need to share your talents and your skills. You are going to need the talents and skills of others. You are going to need meaningful relationships, or you will not make it. Running away to some remote location is extremely foolish and extremely dangerous.

That is why the inner preparation is essential. If you do not know how to read the signs of the world, you will not know what to do in changing circumstances. You will act out of fear or aggression, or you will trust things you should not trust, or you will give yourself over to others who will only lead you into greater danger, or give yourself over to political persuasions that in themselves are a hazard. If you cannot see and cannot know, you will not know what to do, and you will follow others who claim they know what to do, but who in most cases will lead you into greater danger.

God has given you an answer. But you must come to know the answer, live with the answer and apply the answer without changing it, without denying it, without trying to unite it with other things. You must live with it in humility and patience, but with commitment and perseverance as well.

If you fortify yourself and that is all that you do on the outside, others will come to take what you have. If you merely stockpile food and other necessities and that is all that you do, then others will come to take what you have. There is nowhere to run and hide, you see. And when you finally come to realize this, you will recognize you do not have an answer, and perhaps then and only then you will turn to Knowledge. You will pray to God for guidance. You will pray to God for assistance. You will pray to God for deliverance. And perhaps you will have an open mind and realize that without real inner certainty, the certainty that Knowledge can provide, you have no advantages. You have no security. You have no clarity and no certain direction.

If you wait until the evidence is overwhelming, it will be too late for you to make any wise preparations.

This ability to see, to know and to feel the movement of Knowledge—to receive the instruction from Knowledge within yourself and from the signs of the world, which will move you to take action or to reconsider your actions, your behaviors, your goals and your objectives—this is really the turning point.

Today there are increasing numbers of people—many, many people—who are worried about what might happen next. They are genuinely concerned, but they are not moving. They are not moving with Knowledge. They are not preparing for the Great Waves of change. They are just concerned. What will it take to bring them to the point of really taking action, of altering the course of their lives, of changing their objectives? What will it take?

If they can receive the instruction from Knowledge and respond at that level, they will be able to prepare in advance for the Great Waves of change. They will have time to prepare and to make the sometimes difficult changes and adjustments that will be required to reposition themselves—to gain a stronger position, to remove themselves from harm's way, to reduce their vulnerability and thus increase the possibility that they might be of service to others.

But if they wait for the need for change to be overwhelming, it will be too late. Then everyone will panic. Like a herd of beasts in the fields, they will panic. They will run any which way. They will not act with any certainty or any reason. Their actions will be desperate.

If you wait until the evidence is overwhelming, it will be too late for you to make any wise preparations. Then your position will be untenable. Then you will be in a position of extreme powerlessness and vulnerability. Then your options will be very few. There will be no food on the shelves at the stores. The banks will be closed. People will be in panic. It does not take much to create this panic.

You do not want to be in this position. You must act before others act. You must prepare before others prepare. You must go on the strength of Knowledge within yourself and upon the evidence from the world and not upon consensus with other people. For when everyone agrees that the Great Waves of change are upon them, it will be too late to prepare. You must have this strength and this integrity.

As was mentioned at the outset, there are two problems in being able to respond to the movement of Knowledge. The first is simply the inability to respond because your awareness of Knowledge and connection to Knowledge are not yet strong enough for you to feel its movement in your life, to receive its messages and to act upon them.

The second problem is your obligations and commitments to other people. This represents a broad range of situations. Each is somewhat different from the others. But this brings up great problems for many people who may have a family member who is in great trouble or difficulty, and they feel bound and responsible to provide for this person. So how should this be regarded? What are the guidelines here? How should one proceed? Every situation is somewhat unique, and so the guidelines are very general and very broad, but there are a few things you must know at the outset.

In life, your first responsibility is to Knowledge because that is your responsibility to God. That is the responsibility to follow your conscience—to follow your conscience over your ideas, your beliefs, your compromises with others; over your desire for pleasure and your fear of pain; over your acquisition of wealth and fear of poverty—over everything. It is your first responsibility.

Now for this to become a functional reality for you, it will have to be applied in many situations over time, and that is why you need the time to prepare. You do not want to be standing on the beach when the Great Waves come.

But then there is the problem of dependent relationships. This represents a great variety of situations, but beyond the first guideline that your first responsibility is to Knowledge, there are other provisions and circumstances too. It is your responsibility to raise your children to adulthood. You cannot abandon them. You must stay with them. Only in a very extreme situation, if they are highly self-destructive and unmanageable, would you have to part from them. But this would only be in the latter stages of their development and would only be a real exception to the rule.

In life, your first responsibility is to Knowledge.

If you have parents who have no way of supporting themselves, then in certain situations, you will have to provide for them, and that would be a responsibility. This will hold true for many people of course. Do not think in the future that the government or systems of care will provide for the elderly and that you will not have any responsibilities here. Many people will have to face this, and this will have to be part of their preparations.

Then there are situations where you really must serve another person. You are there to serve them. And you must take care of them. Usually, this involves people who are severely disabled, and you will feel that you have a commitment to them. And though it will be difficult and at times extremely trying, you will know that you must stay with them. It will be clear.

Yet in many other cases, the situation is different. If you are in relationship with someone who will not prepare for the Great Waves of change or who demeans you in your attempt to do so, you may well have to leave them and leave them quickly, for they are standing in your way. They are holding you back. They are undermining your progress. They are demeaning you and your relationship with Knowledge. Here you will have to cut the cord, letting people go—not with hostility, but with the certainty that you cannot move forward together.

You cannot get up the mountain if you are staying behind for others.

If you have a spouse or a serious relationship with someone who is mentally disturbed or who is dysfunctional in any way, whether you stay with them or not will be up to Knowledge. But you must be prepared to leave them if that becomes necessary—to protect yourself, to protect your children or to protect your aging parents, whatever your responsibilities require. It is inappropriate for you to be dragged down by someone who will not or cannot move forward in life.

For many people, this represents their first great threshold because it is such a tremendous impediment, and it is holding up their lives already and has been for perhaps a very long time, so they run into this problem immediately in becoming a student of Knowledge. "There is this person in my life that I am bound to, but we are not united. We are not together. And we have established a kind of dependency on one another that is unhealthy."

You must in most cases break free of these situations. Only if Knowledge, the deeper truth within you, makes exception to this should you make exception to this. You cannot move forward if you are held back by others. You cannot get up the mountain if you are staying behind for others—enabling them; supporting them; trying to convince them, persuade them, teach them or change them. You have to break the cord. Life requires it. Knowledge requires it. You know it is true. And it will give you greater strength, it will build your integrity, and it will return self-confidence to you in taking these actions, even if they are very difficult.

If others are destined to fail and are committed to this, you must let them fail. You cannot hold them up. You must let them follow their pathway in life. You are not responsible for them. Only if they represent your children or your aged parents is there an exception to this. But even here, sometimes exceptions have to be made in extreme situations.

If your first responsibility is to Knowledge, then you are free. But freedom must be earned. Freedom must be won. You must overcome the other tendencies in your mind—guilt, obligation, condemnation from others, the need for approval, the need for financial security, the need for social recognition. These now must be overcome as if you were fighting a battle against enemy forces. They must be overcome within yourself. You cannot have everything. You cannot stay where you are and move forward. You cannot win others' approval and follow Knowledge within yourself.

You may praise God. You may worship God. You may fall down on your knees. You may prostrate yourself at the temple. But if you do not carry out what God has given you to do, then you are not honoring God. You are not valuing God. And you are not fulfilling what God has sent you here to do, which in most cases will be very different from your ideas about your life and your notions of fulfillment and happiness.

You must accept that you do not know your greater purpose and give up all attempts at guessing what it might be. It is better to have an open mind and move forward than to entertain great conclusions.

The real question in preparing for the Great Waves is whether you can see them, hear them and feel them and whether you can take the many steps that the preparation may require. Nothing else matters—your political viewpoint, your

You must be free to respond to Knowledge and to move with Knowledge. No idea, no belief, no commitment to others and no other obligation should stand in the way of this.

social standing, your evaluation of yourself, your interests, your hobbies, your friends, your associations, your talents, your skills. If you cannot see, know and respond, none of these things will help you now.

You are entering into greatly uncertain times. Things will be changing increasingly, and sometimes in very unpredictable ways. Knowledge is moving you now, but you must respond to Knowledge to feel what you must do. This book has provided a series of "Recommendations." They will take you very far if you can follow them. Beyond this, you must become a student of Knowledge, learn The Way of Knowledge and follow the power and presence of Knowledge within yourself and within others.

Yet you must be free to respond to Knowledge and to move with Knowledge. No idea, no belief, no commitment to others and no other obligation should stand in the way of this. Perhaps you will think you are being selfish and self-centered, and other people may accuse you of being selfish and self-centered. But if your actions are true, then you are really serving God. You are carrying out the directions that God is providing for you, and you are doing it in such a way that you are not compromising it to meet the needs, expectations or approval of others. Here your freedom to follow the movement of Knowledge will be hard won. Do not think it will be easy, or you will underestimate the opposition, and you will overestimate your promise of success.

God has given you the power and presence of Knowledge. You may ask God for miracles. You may ask God to save you on your sinking ship. You may pray for all number of things. But if you cannot respond to what God has given you, then really your prayers and your invocations are dishonest. They are born of ignorance, arrogance and foolishness. God will not punish you, but you will place yourself in harm's way, and you will face an ever-diminishing set of options and opportunities.

It is to counsel you, to warn you, to encourage you and to prepare you that is the purpose of the New Message. What it is preparing you for is something that is very different from what you have experienced before and on a greater scale—on a scale that is so great you can hardly imagine.

If you think this is just a threat, if you think this is just predicting gloom and doom, then you do not recognize the gift of love that it really is, and you are not yet responsive or responsible to the Greater Power that resides within you that God has put there—to guide you, to bless you and to prepare you.

Now is the time to look, learn, listen and follow. Look at the world. Listen for its signs. Learn what it is teaching you and telling you about what is coming. Begin to prepare your life, to simplify your life, to unburden your life. Everyone can do that right now. Simplify your life. That which is unnecessary—the possessions, the obligations, the ownership, even the relationships that are not essential to you—is only taking energy from you, robbing you of your incentive, distracting you, filling up your time, keeping your eyes off of the world and off your circumstances. You will not see the warning signs before difficult and dangerous things occur if your mind is obsessed with all other things.

So at the very outset, there must be simplification and clarification. Your relationship with any thing, person or place that is not essential or that is counterproductive will rob you of

Your relationship with any thing, person or place that is not essential or that is counterproductive will rob you of vision, energy, purpose and meaning.

vision, energy, purpose and meaning. You can begin with your possessions, and then you will have to review your relationships, your activities and your obligations. Free up your time. Free up your energy to begin to prepare for the Great Waves of change, for they will require tremendous focus and courage from you.

So many people are living where they should not live and engaged in what they should not be engaged in. The wealthy are wasting their time and their lives in meaningless pursuits and acquisitions—wasting the great resources that they have that could be of service to the world and to others, giving themselves to their addictions, indulgences and pleasures at the cost of the focus and the meaning of their lives. In many ways, they are more pathetic than the poorer people, for they show the real waste and insolence that humanity has generated for itself in its destruction of the world, in its destruction of its resources and in its exhaustion of its natural inheritance.

You must begin with the Deep Evaluation, and this evaluation will cover everything in your life.

CHAPTER 5

$\mathcal{T}$he Deep Evaluation

To come to terms with the deeper meaning of your life, the greater purpose of your life, there must be a deep evaluation, and this evaluation will be ongoing. It is fundamentally an evaluation regarding relationships. But I use the word *relationship* here in a more complete sense, for everything that you are associated with represents a relationship—your possessions, your home, your employment, the world itself, the change that is occurring within the world, the nation in which you live and many other things as well. They all represent relationship.

This is a very important way of looking at your involvement in the world, for it gives you a very clear pathway to follow in discerning what is valuable and what is not, what is helpful and what is a hindrance, what will be needed in the future and what will hold you back. Your relationships are not just with people, but with places, with things, with events, with nations and with the whole world itself.

People often do not think of things in the context of relationships, so this is perhaps a new way of looking at the world around you. Its value is that it gives you a very clear discernment, for what works in relationships in one arena can translate into other areas as well. If you have a harmful relationship with your work, for example, it will generate many of the same difficulties and impedance in your life as a difficult relationship with a person. If you have a difficult relationship

You have no neutral relationships, for every one of them is either helping you or hindering you and holding you back.

with your home, it will hold you back. It will limit your possibilities.

You even have a relationship with the future. This is true because you are sent into the world to serve the world as it undergoes the beginning period of great change. You have a relationship with the future. You have a relationship with the past, or with your evaluation of the past, to be more precise.

The condition of your life, then, as a whole represents the condition of all these relationships. And you have no neutral relationships, for every one of them is either helping you or hindering you and holding you back. You are either gaining strength or losing strength in every one of these relationships. Certainly, some are more important and potent than others, but they all have a bearing on your life.

So the deep evaluation is really an evaluation of what you are giving your life to and what you are assigning in life to be your chief influences, for every relationship represents an influence. The power of influence is very significant, but most people are not aware of this or its consequences. Certainly, you can recognize that the person you are married to would have a great influence over you, perhaps the chief influence in your life. But people rarely think, in terms of marriage or partnership, that the other person would become the chief influence in their lives. If this criterion were added to the evaluation of the other person in their relationship and the possibilities for union and partnership with another person, perhaps you would have a very different outcome than what you see in the world today.

So think for a moment in terms of everything being a relationship. You have a relationship with people, places, things, events, the past, the future, world events and your nation. You even have a relationship with the Greater Community of intelligent life in the Universe, though it is unlikely that you have discovered what this means to you yet and how important it will be for your future.

Every relationship represents an influence. The power of influence is very significant.

The next thing to consider is that each of these relationships represents an influence. Each influences you, and you influence them. You have power in the world in this regard, and the world has power over you. The power moves in both directions. And this power gives you the power of decision, which can be applied to more circumstances than you are yet aware of. This power of decision is fundamental to your success and to your future in a world that will be impacted by the Great Waves of change—by environmental destruction, by the decline of your fundamental resources, by a change in the world's climate, by ever-increasing economic and political instability and the great risk of war and conflict that this will produce.

The decisions that are important are the ones you make now, for there is time to prepare for the Great Waves of change. But time is of the essence. You do not have a great deal of time, for already the Great Waves of change are affecting the world. Yet here you stand with all of your relationships and all of their influences upon you.

The great evaluation begins with taking stock of where you are now—how you spend your time, your energy, your focus and your interests. Where is your life being given away? What is it being focused upon? Where is it being assigned? You only have so much energy in the day, so much time in the day, so much space within your mind to consider things. Where is

The decisions that are important are the ones you make now.

that all going now? What are you doing? Who are you with? What are your priorities? Where are you gaining energy in your life, and where are you losing it? And to whom are you losing it, and to what are you losing it? Where do you feel certainty, and where do you feel uncertain? What relationships are you in now that give you a sense of certainty and direction? And which relationships cloud that certainty or obstruct it completely?

As you can see, there are many questions, and these are not all of them. That is why this deep evaluation takes time. It is not something you do in an hour as a process or an exercise. It is not something you spend a weekend thinking about. Instead, it is something you must give yourself to as one of the main priorities of your life, particularly at this time. This should be a major focus for you. For if you do not exercise your focus in this way, if you do not gain a greater discernment, you will not know what to do in the world today or tomorrow. And as the Great Waves of change come, your uncertainty and your vulnerability will increase significantly.

Do not fall into the trap of the dichotomy between being loving versus being fearful. The objective here is to see clearly.

Therefore, you must begin somewhere, and you must begin with where you are—not with what you want, or what you believe, or what you think will happen next, or your goals, or your ambitions or your dreams. Where are you right now? Who are you with, and what are you doing with them? What do you own, and is it giving you strength or taking strength away from you? What do you believe, and are your beliefs giving you clarity, or are they a replacement for Knowledge itself? Where is your time going? Where is your mind going? If you sit in meditation, what is concerning your mind? Where is your mind going? What problems is it solving?

Obviously, this is a very big task and confusing as well because it requires you to become objective about your life. And objectivity here is of central importance. Do not be swayed by the thought that you must be loving as opposed to being fearful, for that is all preferential thinking. It does not represent clarity of mind or real certainty at all. Do not fall into the trap of the dichotomy between being loving versus being fearful. The objective here is to see clearly. The real dichotomy is whether you have wisdom or not, whether you are responsible or not, whether you are preparing for the future or not and whether you are seeing what is coming over the horizon of your life or not.

Begin then with simple things. Review everything that you own. Everything that you own, even insignificant things, have a value to you of some kind and in a subtle way represent an influence. If your life is full of things that have no usefulness or purpose, then they are taking time and energy from you to a certain degree. You still own them, and so you are still in relationship with them. They are occupying space in your home and in your mind. Everything you own really either needs to be fundamentally practical and necessary or personally very meaningful, and that meaning must come in a way that supports who you are now and where you feel you are heading in life.

Things that represent old memories have an influence, drawing you backwards, when in fact you must be facing the future and learning how to live fully in the moment. It is easier to let go of things than to let go of people or to let go of security. So it is a place to begin. The process is one of sorting out, bringing a greater objectivity into your life—looking at every possession that you have and asking, "Is this really useful to me? Is it personally meaningful to me? And does it enhance and strengthen my awareness and understanding of myself?"

You will find that your life is cluttered, that things are weighing you down and that there are a lot of old things in

You want to be flexible, you want to be able to move easily, you do not want to be encumbered by lots of possessions.

your life that perhaps you never think about. But, in reality, they are having an influence over you. As you let them go, you feel lighter and better, and somehow over time your mind becomes clearer. This is a good place to start. It is not very challenging, but it is a beginning step in developing discernment—discernment in relationships—for everything you do, everything you own, and everything you are associated with represents relationships. All of these relationships have an influence upon you—upon your awareness, your decisions and the direction that you know you must follow.

Begin, then, to clear out your life, to simplify. You do not want to carry a lot of extra baggage into the future, for the future will be very uncertain in the face of the Great Waves of change. You want to be flexible, you want to be able to move easily, you do not want to be encumbered by lots of possessions. Here you must be very honest with yourself about what you own and what you do not own, what is meaningful and what is not meaningful.

At the level of Knowledge, it is very clear. It is either a *yes* or a *no*. Or in some cases, there will be neutrality. But regarding things that you own, that you possess and that you are responsible for, generally you will find there will be a *yes* or a *no* within yourself. This will make the decision making very easy, as long as you act upon it, putting away those things that you no longer need or should not own—to be given away or thrown away, whatever the case may require. This is a valuable exercise because you need to free your time and your energy for greater things. Here you are beginning with the simplest things, the simplest relationships, for you will have greater challenges as you proceed.

You are going to need a tremendous amount of energy in the future, and you must gather your resources together. You must gather your strength and build your focus. If your time and life are being spent mindlessly in all directions, you will not have the power to do this, for power here represents concentration. If your life is not focused and concentrated, then your energy is being lost in many different places. Now you must plug up the gaps. Now you must reclaim what is being lost. Now you must gather together all of your strength, for you will need it for the difficult times ahead. You will need it to override and overcome the other influences in your life that are dissuading you and holding you back from doing what you know you must do and from discerning a greater direction that Knowledge within you is attempting to provide for you as you go along.

This deep evaluation continues on to greater things: to your work, to your relationships, to your relationship with your body and to your relationship with your mind. Here it is more difficult to bring objectivity because you can identify with these things far more. Identifying with things means that you lose your objectivity regarding them. To review your work, to review your relationships and to review your relationship with your mind and your body, which represents your relationship with yourself, require a very great objectivity. But at the level of Knowledge, the response is fundamental.

For example, in your relationships, you must review every one of them to see if they are helping you or hindering you, if the people you are involved with are moving forward in life. In some circumstances, in your employment

Power here represents concentration. If your life is not focused and concentrated, then your energy is being lost in many different places.

for example, you may have to work with people regardless, but how you engage with them will make a big difference in the impact they will have upon your life.

Regarding relationships that you choose and select for yourself, you must evaluate each one: "Is this relationship strengthening me or weakening me? Is this person moving in the direction that I must move? Do we have a greater destiny together, or should I release this person to follow their own journey in life?"

One person in your life can hold you back and alter the destiny and course of your life.

These are valuable questions. You must gain the strength, the courage and the objectivity to ask them and to act upon them. One person in your life can hold you back and alter the destiny and course of your life. You should never underestimate the power of influence in your relationships. Even if it is a casual friendship, this friendship is either helping you or hindering you in moving forward. As you begin to take steps in moving forward, you will see very soon if this friendship is helping you or hindering you, if the other person is questioning you, belittling you or doubting you in your efforts to focus your life and to prepare yourself for the future.

You will need strong companions. You cannot afford to have detractors in your life. You can learn from their challenges, but if you associate with them closely, you will lose ground to them.

Here developing strength and discernment will take time and can be very difficult in certain circumstances, for there are people whose approval you think you must have. There are people you are still trying to impress. There are people who you think you need for safety, for security, for love or for pleasure. But at the level of Knowledge, it will be *yes* or *no*, for Knowledge is trying to take you somewhere, and everyone and everything in your life is either helping you or hindering you in discovering and following this direction.

You will need strong companions.

Your employment either has a future or not in the face of the Great Waves of change. That is something that you can evaluate intellectually. Yet at the level of Knowledge, it is still a *yes* or a *no*. Perhaps you will need to stay in this employment for a time, to give you stability while you make other decisions and while you gain a greater certainty about where you must go and the next steps you must follow in your life. But do not over commit yourself to a situation that has no future, that will not be able to exist in the great difficulties to come.

Do not over commit yourself to anyone or anything until you have fulfilled this deep evaluation. Do not make any great plans. Do not try to rechart the course of your life. Do not commit yourself in marriage or relationship until you have undertaken this deep evaluation over time.

Do not give your life away before you know what your life is for and the direction that it must follow. If you will follow this, it will save you. For it is so easy to give your life away to others—to commit yourself to a line of work or to establish a set of circumstances that will prevent you from ever realizing and remembering your greater purpose for coming into the world.

People establish relationships casually, using very weak and temporary criteria. They do not realize the seriousness of their engagements and the impact that it has upon them. It is because they lack discernment. It is because they do not value their lives that they would give themselves away so easily and commit their time and

Do not give your life away before you know what your life is for and the direction that it must follow. If you will follow this, it will save you.

energy without greater care, that they would be so careless with themselves.

This is a very important part of the deep evaluation. You cannot follow your intellect in this, for there are always good reasons to give yourself to things that will never be valuable to you. There are always compelling reasons to give your life away to people or to circumstances that do not represent your destiny.

Then there are social forces that encourage you to marry before you are ready, to have a family before you are ready, to commit yourself to a career before you are ready. All the social forces—the forces from your family and the encouragement from your friends—so often lead you completely in the wrong direction for your life. Do not condemn your family and friends, for they do not know. But you must know. You must gain this Knowledge. And the Knowledge that God has given you makes this possible. Otherwise, you would become lost in the world and would never find your way.

There are always compelling reasons to give your life away to people or to circumstances that do not represent your destiny.

Your relationship with your mind and your body represents a very great teaching that the New Message provides. Your mental health and your physical health are important. But to deal with them effectively, you must bring the same objectivity to them. Of course, you identify with your mind and your body, even to the extent that you think that that is who you are. But your mind is not who you are, and your body is not who you are. Instead, they represent vehicles of expression—vehicles through which you can participate in the world, have an influence in the world and express yourself and communicate to others in the world.

They are vehicles to take you somewhere, to take you through life in this world, to live at this time, to have an impact upon this time. They are vehicles. Therefore, you must care for them. You must cultivate them, and they must be able to enable you to fulfill your mission in the world. If your health is broken down, either mentally or physically, you will not be able to follow a greater purpose, and in most cases it will never be revealed to you because you are not ready to follow it.

If you do not set a real direction in your life, other people will set the direction for you.

Getting your life in order, then, involves also addressing the needs for your health—your mental health and your physical health. The mind requires some structure. It requires enjoyment. It requires companionship. And it requires relief and rest. You are able to discern this through your activities, through the influences you bring into your home, through the media, through your relationships, through the books you read and the things that you think about.

Most people have never developed any control over their minds. They are simply the unwitting slaves to whatever their mind wants to think about, and so they feel very helpless in this regard. But in the deep evaluation, which is a process of bringing clarity and objectivity into your life, you are able to gain greater and greater control over your mind and thinking by deciding what you will think about, what you will respond to, what you will listen to, what you will read, what will be in your home, what will be the focus of your activities and so forth. You must gain this control because if you do not control your mind, other people will. If you do not set a real direction in your life, other people will set the direction for you. This, indeed, is the tragic circumstance of most of the people in the world today, whether they be rich or poor.

It is obvious that those who are greatly impoverished are

slaves to their circumstances. But it is not so obvious that those who are more affluent, and even the very wealthy, are also slaves to their circumstances. Though they have great enjoyments and freedom of time, in the end they are as lost and as deprived as the poorest around them. They will not fare well in facing the Great Waves of change that are coming to the world. They have no advantage. Their wealth can be lost easily, and they will be the target of other people, who will prey upon them. And they will live in great fear and anxiety—afraid to lose what they have and afraid of everyone and everything that they believe can take away from them their pleasures, their freedoms or their opportunities.

Here you are gaining strength and learning to become inner-directed rather than merely being outer-directed.

This is the time, then, to recognize what is needed for your mind and what is needed for your body—very simply. Nothing complex here. If you are following Knowledge, nothing is complex here. You have simple guidelines, and you must adhere to them.

At the outset, regarding your deep evaluation, whether it be regarding your possessions, your relationships, your activities or your engagements, it will be important for you to create space in your life to let things go, to open up your life, to allow there to be space in your life without it being filled by something else. In doing so, you will see how much you have tried to gain certainty through your ownership of things, through your relationships, through your engagements and so forth. You will perhaps feel less certain about your life and more vulnerable, but this is a good thing, for this creates a space for a Greater Power to fill and the freedom for you to set a new course, which will bring new people and circumstances into your life. If your life is already filled to the brim, nothing new can come. There can be no new experiences, no new revelations, no new relationships, no new opportunities.

So at the outset, the deep evaluation is a process of discernment and release. You are discerning what is really important and releasing that which is not important. You are changing your relationship with things, with people, with places and with engagements. In so doing, you are changing, on a subtle but increasingly powerful level, your relationship with your mind and your body. Here you are gaining strength and learning to become inner-directed rather than merely being outer-directed.

Many people ask, "Well, what shall I do in the face of the Great Waves of change?" Begin with this deep evaluation. That is fundamental. If this is not undertaken, you will not be free to know, you will not be free to act and you will not be free to move with Knowledge. You will be held in place, as if you were chained to a wall—unable to move, unable to reconsider your life and unable to set a new direction. For your life will already have been committed away, given over to others, or just simply lost in the countless thoughts and pursuits that you carry on in the course of your life.

You begin with the deep evaluation, and this evaluation continues. It is ongoing because bringing clarity, simplicity and focus to your life is ongoing. You do not do it all at once. It is ongoing. Everything around you wants to encumber you even more with possessions, with people, with places, with opportunities, with distractions, with stimulation and so forth. And so this discernment continues on because you must keep your life open, clear and uncluttered. Your life must be filled with people, places and things that strengthen you, that encourage you and that are symbolic that you have the strength and the responsibility to

Here you will have to learn to say no to many things: no even to your own mind.

live fully in the moment and to prepare for the future in a way that is wise and effective.

Here you will have to learn to say *no* to many things: *no* even to your own mind; *no* to your compulsions; *no* to your addictions; *no* to those pleasures that hurt your mind and your body; *no* to people who want you to do what they want you to do; *no* to opportunities that look good, but which, at a deeper level, you cannot accept; *no* to the consensus of people around you; *no* you will not follow their advice; *no* you will not join their group; *no* you will not accept their perception of reality. You do this not with anger or condemnation, not with fear of rejection, but with simple honesty and simple clarity.

Do not be angry that the world is full of deception and full of dishonesty because it is a world without Knowledge. People have not found God's great gift yet, and so they act foolishly, mimicking one another, following whatever their social conditioning tells them they must follow—following their friends, their groups, their leaders, their religions—everything. For without Knowledge, what else could they do but follow everything that is a substitute for Knowledge?

This should not be a source of anger for you if you are seeing it clearly. It is tragic, yes. It is greatly unfortunate, yes. But you cannot afford to be a critic of the world now. Instead of condemning others, condemning the governments, condemning the world, condemning life, you must draw your resources to you. All of that condemnation represents a huge loss of energy, a loss of energy that only adds more friction and complaint to life, without any positive benefit. If your life is not moving with Knowledge, then your position as a critic is pointless and self-defeating. This is part of the conservation of your energy.

In the end, the great evaluation returns strength to you, connects you with Knowledge and conserves your energy. Perhaps you do not yet see the value of conserving your energy, for you want every moment of your life to be filled with pleasant stimulation, with meaningful activities, with enjoyable people. You want to fill up the space, but you need to open up the space, allowing it to be empty, holding it in reserve. For it is only in this space that new realizations come to you and that you are able to see things you could not see before, to know things you could not know before, to discern things that were beyond your reach before. New people and new opportunities come into your life because there is a space for them. So, in essence, your life must always have this space and this openness. It should never be filled up. And if it does become filled up, then it is time to let things go once again.

Instead of trying to fill up the space, you want to create the space and maintain a part of your life as open, unexplained and mysterious.

Even if your life were completely engaged appropriately, even if you were living The Way of Knowledge, even if every person in your life were meaningful to you and were a proponent of Knowledge within you and for you, you would still have to create an opening—this space in your life where nothing exists, where there is emptiness. It is this emptiness that allows you to be still, allows you to listen, allows you to look, allows you to really be with another person, to really experience a place and to enjoy the magnificence of nature. It is this space, this emptiness, this silence that allow you to discern the signs of the world and the movement of Knowledge within yourself.

Instead of trying to fill up the space, you want to create the space and maintain a part of your life as open, unexplained and mysterious. Nothing is going on there. It is this that allows you to have wonder and reverence towards life, to have a pure experience instead of something that simply stimulates your thinking. It creates the opportunity for you to experience yourself outside of time and place—the experience of Grace, the experience of your Unseen Teachers, who are helping you to regain your connection with Knowledge and with it your greater purpose for coming into the world.

You can imagine here that if you followed this through, your home would have very few things in it, but everything in it would be very valuable. Your personal life would have very few people in it, but every person would be really valuable. Your time would not be filled up, but would have openings in it for new experiences to happen. And your mind would not be constantly stimulated, but would be able to become quiet, observant and sensitive—seeing, hearing, recognizing things.

It is like you are going in the opposite direction from the majority of people around you, who are all about acquiring things for themselves—possessions, people, experiences, sensations, stimulation—to the point where they have no idea who they are. Their life is filled up with external stimulation. They have no sense of where they are in life, where they are going or where the world is going. They are simply being swept away by all of their obsessions.

You can imagine, then, as a result of this deep evaluation, that your life becomes simple and clear and that you are able to discern opportunities at a more fundamental level—not whether they are pleasing and exciting, but whether they are truly meaningful and whether they serve your purpose or distract you from it.

You will certainly be able to have simple pleasures along the way, but anything that requires a more serious engagement—a new relationship, an important possession, an opportunity in your work, a new interest—these things must really be discerned because the whole world wants you to fill yourself up, while you, in essence, are trying to empty yourself out. This is why you must have very limited exposure to the media, only looking for those things that are important regarding the Great Waves of change or in some cases that are important in your immediate circumstances and environment.

You should not be stimulated by the world. You are going to have to maintain some distance now if you are ever to have a hope of gaining your strength, building your discernment, cultivating your discretion and learning to become really observant—really being able to see what you need to see in yourself and in others. You cannot do this if you are running around like a crazy person—driven by your needs and desires and obligations to others. That is why the deep evaluation must happen at the outset if you are to have any chance of success. And this evaluation will continue, for there are thresholds that you must evaluate for yourself.

The whole world wants you to fill yourself up, while you, in essence, are trying to empty yourself out.

Part of this you will undertake on your own, and part of it will be assisted by other people. The quality of your relationships now will become ever more important to you as you recognize that each relationship is significant in its influence upon you—whether it supports the emergence of Knowledge within you or whether it distracts you from this emergence, whether it encourages your preparation for the Great Waves of change or whether it discourages this preparation. Your relationships here are of the greatest importance, and this importance will grow over time.

As you proceed, then, your life will have greater resources of energy. You will be able to undertake significant change in your life—change that you could not undertake before because you did not have the strength to do it. You did not have the potency within yourself to carry it through. Before, you saw things you knew you needed to do, but you did not have the strength to do them. You could not override your own mind or the opinions of others. You were just not strong enough to do it. Now you can do it, and it is giving your life greater flow and greater movement.

Can you imagine that everything in your life represents your greater purpose in the world, the greater meaning of your life and that this has given you enough strength that you can deal with adversity now? It does not defeat you. You can deal with others disagreeing with you or criticizing you without losing yourself to their viewpoints.

Allow yourself to be with the discomfort. Feel it. See what it is telling you. See where it is taking you.

This is a source of fulfillment and joy in your life. It is like you have been reclaimed. You have reclaimed yourself, and you have allowed others to come into your life who support that reclamation, which is fundamentally the reclamation of Knowledge.

Along the way, you have gained skills that you can now use to assist others, for they too must begin the deep evaluation. They too must learn how to gain their own strength and to reclaim their lives, which had been given away before without thought or consideration. The tools that you gain, the strength that you gain, the skills that you employ all become resources for assisting others in the future, and you will do this naturally, spontaneously. Even your life will be a demonstration of this, which will inspire and confuse other people.

The truth is you are not where you need to be in life, and you know this, and that is why you are uncomfortable. Do not try to get rid of the discomfort, for it is a sign within you that your life must move, that there is change that must be brought about, and that you must do it. Allow yourself to be with the discomfort. Feel it. See what it is telling you. See where it is taking you. Where are the points of discomfort? Where is the lie being lived in your life? What are the mistruths you are telling yourself about your relationship with this person, this place or this thing?

You will have to overcome tendencies within yourself, habits within yourself and the other voices that the world around you has put in your mind, telling you that you want things you really do not want, or that you must have things to be attractive or to be successful.

This is a very great process. The truth remains that you are not where you need to be. Do not ever tell yourself you are just where you need to be. That is foolishness. You will never convince Knowledge within yourself.

You have a great mountain to climb, and you must keep moving up this mountain to fulfill your destiny and to gain a vision of the world, which will become obvious to you once you reach the higher altitudes of this mountain.

Whatever you tell yourself, you cannot convince Knowledge within yourself. You need to get to where you need to be—to be in the best position for the future, to reclaim your strength, your skills and your greater gifts and to be of service to a world whose needs will only grow and become more profound in the future.

CHAPTER 6

Relationships and the Great Waves

YOU HAVE FOUR PILLARS IN YOUR LIFE, the Pillars that uphold your life. They give it strength, balance and certainty. These are the Pillar of Relationships, the Pillar of Work, the Pillar of Health and the Pillar of your Spiritual Development. Like the four legs of a table, they uphold your life. The strength of your life and the ability of your life to undergo change and uncertainty depend in great part upon these Pillars. While you have Knowledge, the deeper intelligence that God has given you to guide you, to protect you and to lead you to your greater accomplishments, the emphasis must still be on building these Four Pillars.

This chapter discusses the Pillar of Relationships. This includes all of your relationships, how you participate in relationships, your strengths and weaknesses in relationships, the quality of relationships that you have with others—who in your life is strengthening you and who in your life is making you weaker. This primarily is regarding your relationship with individuals, but in a more complete sense, it also includes your relationship with your possessions, your home, your mind, your body, your nation, the Earth, your relationship with nature and so forth. This Teaching will focus on your relationship with individuals because they have the greatest impact upon your thinking, awareness and abilities.

It must be understood at the outset that the quality of your relationships with others will largely determine the kind of life you will have, what will be available to you, the vision you will have and the degree of courage you will have to follow the movement of Knowledge within yourself. Here Knowledge cannot move you in your life. It cannot guide you or protect you if your Pillars are too weak. In this case, if there are people who depend upon you remaining as they want you to be, who are afraid of any kind of change or emergence within your life, who would suspect or denounce any kind of deeper inclination you might have to the degree that it would threaten their interest in you, they will hold you back. They will influence you. They will discourage you. They will cast doubt upon you even if they are wonderful and loving people. If they do not recognize the reality of the deeper nature within themselves, then they will regard it within you with suspicion and uncertainty. They will not trust it. They will not know it. It will seem strange, confusing and threatening to them. And whatever they are doing with you in life will seem to be cast in doubt.

Who you are with and who is influencing you has a great bearing on what you will know and your ability to follow what you know.

Who you are with and who is influencing you has a great bearing on what you will know and your ability to follow what you know, the ability to follow the greater intelligence that God has placed within you. Contemplating the Great Waves of change that are coming to the world, the very difficult reality of comprehending humanity's emergence into the Greater Community of life in the Universe and the Intervention that is occurring in the world today will show you who amongst your friends and relatives will support you in this inquiry and who will share this interest with you. Not everyone who encourages you will share this interest, so they do not need to have this interest to support you. But you will see at the outset who will stand with you and who will oppose you, who will discourage you and who will encourage you. This is very important to see.

People are often shocked to discover that their closest friends or their nearest relatives really did not support the emergence of Knowledge or their entertaining deeper questions about their lives and about the world. They were such good friends on a personal level, but beyond that level, they had so little in common. It is as if they didn't really know each other at all. They only shared interests and hobbies and simple innocuous dialogue, but beyond that there was not a deeper connection between them.

One of the first great thresholds you will have to face is sharing with others your awareness of the Great Waves of change, your inquiry into the Greater Community of life and your focus on building your connection to the mystery and the power of Knowledge within yourself. Be prepared, for the response may not be what you want it to be. That is to be expected, for if your closest friends and your closest relatives really supported Knowledge within you, they would have been doing it all along. It would have been a focus in their relationship with you. They would have encouraged it. They would have encouraged you to be true to yourself, to search your feelings and to discern your deeper inclinations. If that has not been the case, then it is likely that they will not support your deeper inquiry now, and they will not understand what you are doing and why you are concerning yourself with such difficult and important questions.

Here you must be willing to continue even if others fall away. And in certain cases, you will have to leave even long-standing relationships, for they can only hinder you now in your greater journey. They can only pull you back to the way you used to be, the way they want you to be, the way they are used to your being. But do not condemn them for this, for they do not yet have the awareness. Yet be grateful that the awareness is coming to you because this gives you time to learn and to prepare, and perhaps one day you will be able to help them in their inquiry. But at the outset, you must gain your own strength. You are not strong enough to teach others and to encourage others. You do not have the skill. You do not have the certainty. You have not traveled far enough up this mountain to be able to guide others, even at the outset.

You have to find out within the context of the world why you are really here. What are your gifts? What does the world need from you specifically that you are equipped to provide?

Here you must be willing to journey alone and face loneliness because it is better to be alone than it is to be engaged in relationships that cannot journey with you in The Way of Knowledge. It is better to face loneliness than it is to engage with people who really have nothing to offer you—no wisdom, no encouragement and no insight. Before, you were really just spending your time mindlessly, and now you must spend it wisely. And relationships take a great deal of time.

Here you will be looking for deeper qualities in people. Beauty, charm and wittiness will be seen as having no real value now. You want depth and honesty. You want earnestness. You want clarity. You are looking for a deeper resonance with others. You want others who are looking at the world, responding to the world and who are beginning to respond to Knowledge as you are beginning to respond to Knowledge. You want people who can resonate with you and encourage you now, for you will need this.

Breaking free of others who cannot do this and breaking free compassionately and wisely is not easy. In some cases, it will seem heart wrenching. It will be so confusing to you that they cannot see what you see and feel what you feel and know what you know. Not only are they not experiencing these things, they will not even seem to value them. They will say, "What is wrong with you? You used to be such a fun person, and now you are so serious. Why are you concerning yourself with these things? It is too fearful. It is too extreme." They will question your motives. They will question your insights. They will weaken your confidence.

Nearly everyone has to face this at the outset, and sometimes it can be very disappointing. Yet you still must journey on. You have a greater purpose in life to discover. You have to take the steps to Knowledge. You have to find out within the context of the world why you are really here. What are your gifts? What does the world need from you specifically that you are equipped to provide? You have a greater journey to take now. It will change your relationships, it will change your priorities, and it will change what you look for in other people.

This is entirely natural. This is the result of growing up. Even if there were no Great Waves of change, even if humanity remained isolated in the Universe, you would still have to take these great steps to mature as a person—to build character within yourself, to learn about your mind and your inclinations, your strengths and your weaknesses and to embark upon a deeper evaluation of your life.

The Great Waves of change add tremendous urgency to this deep evaluation, but in and of itself, it is an entirely natural and necessary process. That others are not responding does not mean that it is not meant for you. That others are not growing up does not mean that you should not grow up. That others are remaining foolish, ignorant and self-obsessed is not a reason for you to do the same.

You are both blessed and burdened now—blessed because you have been forewarned, blessed because the spark of Knowledge has been ignited within you, blessed because at last after so many years of searching and emptiness, you are beginning to find something—something you can experience and follow, something that will give you a greater direction and a greater connection to life.

Yet it is also a burden. For now you must consider things that you would not consider before. Now you must look courageously out into the world, and you must look courageously within yourself. You must begin the great evaluation, and you must be willing in life to chart a different course—not a course that you have fantasized about, not a course that represents your former goals and ideals, but something deeper and more genuine, something natural to you, but at the same time something with which you are unfamiliar.

Here you are not creating your reality. You are allowing your reality to emerge within you. You will have to create a place for it to emerge. You will have to create an environment for it to emerge, but its emergence is natural and essential for you, for this is who you really are. Beyond your personality, beyond your beliefs and ideas, beyond your memories of the past, this represents your greater identity that is now beginning to emerge in your life. It has been called because you have reached a point in your life where it becomes necessary, and you are being called by the world, for the world is calling you. The signs of the world are calling you to prepare—to awaken from your dreams of self-fulfillment, to prepare for the Great Waves of change and to prepare for the Greater Community.

This is a very important point, you see, because while the answer is within you, the calling is not. It is beyond you. It is out in the world. What calls you to a greater purpose is out in the world. The answer to this calling is within you, but the calling is out there. Because the Great Waves of change are coming and are beginning to influence and affect the lives of ever-increasing numbers of people, the calling of the world is there. It is powerful. It is engaging. It is essential.

That is why you are responding now. That is why you have been feeling a greater sense of anxiety about the future and a greater concern for what you are here to do in your life, what is really important in your life and what you are here to accomplish. It is this calling, you see. You have been feeling it for some time, and now the revelation of the New Message is showing you what you are experiencing. It is bearing witness to your experience. It is advocating for this experience to increase and to emerge within you. It is a confirmation of Knowledge within yourself and what you yourself must learn to see, to know and to do for this Knowledge to emerge and to express itself fully through you.

While the answer is within you, the calling is not. It is beyond you. It is out in the world.

This is not a time to look for romance. This is not a time to try to get married. This is not a time to commit yourself to someone or to a set of circumstances because you are building a fundamental relationship with yourself, and you are undertaking a deep evaluation of your life. It is better now that there be no one else competing for your attention. If someone is, it will make this evaluation far more difficult and confuse your situation terribly. Even if they are the right person for you, they must wait. And if they are the right person, they will wait.

You need time now to get your bearings, to see where you are, to see what you know, to evaluate your relationships with people, places and things and to discern the direction that you must follow. There should be no one else competing for your attention, and you should hold yourself back. Do not give yourself over now. That would be a terrible mistake. It would be bypassing an essential step in your life.

If you are a person who has relied upon being in relationship with others, this might seem difficult—to be on your own like this, to withhold your affections, to keep yourself out of any kind of intimate engagement with anyone. If someone is trying to seduce you or to overcome your inclinations, if someone is trying to persuade you to be in relationship with them, then you can be sure that they do not respect the deeper movement of your life. This will likely mean that they are not appropriate for you, either now or at any time. Do not let anyone's desires or expectations overtake you now. You must have this restraint. You must establish these boundaries.

You will need time, and quite a bit of time actually, to discern your real direction. There should be no distractions from this—no one pulling you to the side, no one pulling you back, no one trying to win you over, no one trying to encourage you to be in relationship with them. No distractions. If you are going to take this great step in your life, there must be no distractions.

You must establish this foundation within yourself before you can commit yourself to anyone or anything.

If you are in a relationship with someone now, you may have to withdraw for a period of time. If they can support this, that is good. If they cannot support it, then you know that they will not be able take this journey with you, regardless of your affection for each other, regardless of what you have created together. Fundamentally, they will not move in the direction in which you must now move, and there is nothing you can do about it.

This is where Knowledge becomes your first responsibility. Before, you were giving your life away to other people. You were giving your life away to your own desires. You were giving your life away to your own fears. You were giving your life away to what the culture was telling you that you should be, do and have. But now you are allowing Knowledge within yourself to set the direction, to set the boundaries, to say *yes* to this and *no* to that, to give you clarity, to give you back to yourself and to give you a direction and steps to follow.

For some people, this will be the most difficult threshold, and many will not pass through this threshold. They will turn away from Knowledge. They will turn away from the signs of the world and the signs of their own deeper experience to protect what they have, to please the one they are trying to please, to hold on to their financial security, to hold on to their social position. They will fall back into the shadows, and Knowledge will remain latent within them—waiting for the moment when it might emerge again, waiting for the time when they will question their assumptions, their attachments and their commitments.

But for you, you must establish this foundation within yourself before you can commit yourself to anyone or anything. Your first priority is to become strong with Knowledge and to engage yourself in a deep evaluation about your life, relationships and activities. In your heart, you know this to be true. If you feel you have been alone and have done this evaluation, and yet you do not have a clear direction, if you do not know what steps to follow, then you have not really done this. You have just been alone.

Perhaps you are not asking the right questions or listening deep enough for the power and presence of Knowledge within yourself. Perhaps you are not looking at the Great Waves of change. Perhaps the idea of humanity's emergence into the Greater Community had never occurred to you, or you only thought about it occasionally. Whatever the case may be, the deep evaluation must be deep enough to be effective. It must be substantial, and it must show you what is coming over the horizon of the world, for this will give you certainty. This will give you motivation, for you will realize you cannot stay where you are. You are not living in the past anymore. The world that you are accustomed to will change dramatically. You cannot rest on any former presumptions or assurances. There is no safe and secure place to hide from the vicissitudes of life now.

If you can face this, you will gain courage. If you can face this without denial, without preference, without projecting your own ideas, hopes and wishes, you will gain clarity and objectivity. Courage, clarity and objectivity—so rare they are in the human experience, and yet so absolutely necessary to provide certainty, direction and balance in one's life.

It is better to be with one person who will encourage you than it is to have a whole host of friends and family around you who have no idea what is moving your life. You must face this. You must have the strength to say *no* to others. You must have the courage to carry on the deep evaluation of your life. Otherwise, you will not know yourself. You will not know your experience. And you will be too afraid to look out over the horizon.

This is the condition of so many people, especially the wealthy people. They really do not want to look out on the horizon. Most of them are too afraid of how they must change, what they must let go of, what they must reconsider—so engulfed they are in their pursuit of happiness and pleasure, wealth and power. It is very sad. Their wealth has done nothing for them and, in fact, has made them weaker and less able to respond to life.

Therefore, do not envy them. Their tragedy is not something you want to have. In the future, owning a lot of things will be a real burden. Having great wealth will be a real burden. How will you protect it? How much will it govern your life? The Great Waves will create a set of circumstances that will make being very wealthy extremely hazardous, with all those hungry faces looking at you. No, no, that is not the way.

You will need great companions in The Way of Knowledge. You will need others who are strong enough to face the Great Waves of change and who are willing to begin to look ahead at the Greater Community and humanity's future and destiny there. You must have others who are beginning to take the same kind of journey you are taking.

This is not about romance and marriage now. That may

come later. That is not the emphasis now. Break the addiction to romance. Do not become sexually engaged with anyone during this initial period. Do not give yourself away to anyone. You will have to bring everything to bear here—all of your attention. It must be the great focus of your life. That is how serious it is, and that is what is required. In time, others will come to join you.

It is better to be with one person who will encourage you than it is to have a whole host of friends and family around you who have no idea what is moving your life.

You will be tempted by romance. You will be tempted by relationship, beauty, charm and wealth. They will all still have certain degrees of attraction for you. But Knowledge within you will not be impressed at all by them and will not respond to them. And the stronger you are with Knowledge, the more immune you become to these seductions and attractions.

But you are not there yet. You must take this journey to gain that strength, that immunity and that freedom. Oh, what a freedom it is to be free from seduction. When you are free, everyone else looks like they are in chains, like they are slaves to their wishes, their desires, their fears and their inappropriate engagements with other people. But to gain this freedom requires a kind of struggle within yourself and real self-determination.

Beyond the sphere of your personal relationships, you will need to gain the expertise of people who are looking at the Great Waves—people who have different skills, different talents, different professions. You will need to learn about the Great Waves—what they really mean, how they are unfolding. What are the possible outcomes for humanity? You must do this with as much objectivity as possible. It does not have to become an obsessive investigation, but it is part of your education overall.

Therefore, you will have to become a student of the world as well as a student of Knowledge—studying what is really important. What is really important for you to study now, regarding the world in all of its conflicts and distractions, all of its seductions and tragedies? What should you be looking for there?

There are a few things that are important. You must become aware of situations around the world regarding the availability of food and water. You must become aware of changes in climate and its effect upon food production in the world and its effect upon the well-being of people in both urban and rural environments. You must be aware of political and economic instability and how it is manifesting in certain places. You must be aware of the outbreaks of pandemic illnesses. And you must be aware of conflicts that continue to exist and conflicts that may emerge in the future. When you look at the world, look for these things. Just bear witness to them and see if there are any signs. Not everything you will look at is important. Not everything you look at will be a sign.

You look and you watch with Knowledge, which is looking without preference or judgment. It is just looking. You listen without preference or judgment. It is just listening. If you find a real sign, it will impress itself upon you particularly. It will not just be an emotional response of sadness or grief, remorse or anger. It will be something that will ring within you. That is important. Write it down—what you heard, where you heard it, how it impressed you. And stay with that, for a sign is more important than stimulation.

You look for the signs. You do not have to become an expert in any of these areas. You do not have to study them in depth. But you need to look into them for the signs. For the signs will tell you how quickly the Great Waves are approaching. They will tell you how much time you have to carry out the things that you are trying to do even right now.

Like the animals in the field and the birds in the air, you are watching and listening for changes in your environment. While others continue to be preoccupied and self-obsessed, carefree and careless, you must pay attention, and that is why there can be no competition for your attention now. Romance and relationship must wait. You must create space within your mind to listen, to look and to learn. You must slow your life down so that you can listen, look and learn. Beginning *Steps to Knowledge* will teach you how to still your mind and how to listen more deeply within your own experience, looking for the signs.

Like the animals in the field and the birds in the air, you are watching and listening for changes in your environment.

It is your relationship with Knowledge now that is so fundamental and that must take precedence over any other relationship that you have. Even your children who will stay with you, even they cannot interfere with your relationship with Knowledge. The more that you build this relationship, the more you will be able to share it with your children and encourage it in them. For you can never be too young to learn about Knowledge—to learn how to recognize your deeper experience and be true to yourself.

This is the way that God has laid out. It has always been this way. Religion and all of its emphasis and tragedy, the infusion of culture and history and the manipulation of leaders and institutions have not changed the fundamental nature of God's Revelation—which is Knowledge within the individual and, through Knowledge, contribution to the world. It is fundamental. This is at the heart of every religion. Take away the miracles, take away the pageantry, take away the institutional guidelines, and you have the mystery of Knowledge within yourself, waiting to be discovered.

Now the world is calling for this, for Great Waves of change are upon the world, and humanity is now facing Intervention from the Greater Community itself. The world is forcing an advancement in human evolution. The world is calling Knowledge out of you, and it must respond. This is the power of your time, and it will give you work to do that will be fundamental and necessary, both within yourself and in the world.

CHAPTER 7

Preparing Your Family

PREPARING FOR THE GREAT WAVES OF CHANGE requires
many things. It is important, if you have a family and are
married, that you begin to prepare them as well. Your young
children do not need to know what is coming, but your spouse
or your partner must become educated and supportive of your
efforts. This is very important because where you live and how
you live—your occupation, where you are situated, your
transportation—all of this will be very important.

Many people, even in affluent nations, are very poorly
positioned for this, of course, and because it takes such a long
time to come to terms with this emotionally and then to begin to
make the necessary adjustments in one's life, the sooner this
preparation can begin, the better. Again, time is of the essence.
If you have very little time, you will have very few options, and
you may not be able to do much at all.

If your spouse or partner is reluctant or uncertain, then you
must still make the necessary preparations. You must become a
leader here. You must assume responsibility. Your children
should know, at least, that nature has been harmed by human
misuse and by human greed. People have used too much of the
natural resources, and now there is less to go around.

In your family, pleasures should be simple, and you must
focus on your economy, saving as much of your financial
resources for the future as you possibly can, following the
"Recommendations" that are included in this book and

beginning to learn The Way of Knowledge so that the power of guidance that God has placed within you may be known to you and available to you. Others will now be depending upon your taking concerted action.

It is a great challenge to be the one who is awakened while others are still sleeping and dreaming.

Therefore, you do not have much time for doubt and ambivalence in this matter. Your family then becomes a great incentive for you to learn about the Great Waves, to develop your connection to Knowledge and to take the initial steps that are recommended.

Your older children should really become educated about the Great Waves. Let them read. Direct them to resources that can help to educate them. Have meaningful and objective conversations with them. If they are reluctant or do not want to know, you must still lead your family. Again, do not rely upon consensus.

If there is severe disagreement between you and your spouse, or partner, regarding the change that must be made, then you must still be the leader. If you are clear and if Knowledge is directing you, you must be the leader, and you must take whatever actions are necessary to protect your family and your children, with or without your spouse's participation. You cannot be held back now by anyone, for the times demand recognition and preparation.

If you have elderly parents, depending upon their circumstances and condition, you may not be able to educate them. But you will have to plan for how they can be cared for, given whatever resources are available. This can be a very difficult matter, and you may need to seek professional advice.

It is a great challenge to be the one who is awakened while others are still sleeping and dreaming. It can be a great challenge to be the one who sees, knows and feels the great change that is coming while others remain numb or turn their backs. Yet this is your preparation—not only for the world to come, not only for the future, but also your preparation to become strong, to guide others and to take greater responsibilities in your life. Do not reject or resent this. It is necessary, and it will be redeeming for you. As it has been said, the Great Waves of change are accelerating a process that must take place anyway. It is necessary for you to grow up, to become objective, to become observant, to become aware of your environment and to become aware of your connection to the future and your relationship with the future.

In your preparation, you must minimize expenses as much as possible, even if you are affluent. You are going to need these resources in the future. Your pleasures and activities should be simple, for you will need to preserve your energy and your resources now. Do not think that your financial position or your financial status will be preserved into the future in the face of the Great Waves of change. That would be a very grave mistake. For in the future, many people will be unemployed, will not have work and will be financially desperate and destitute. Even governments in the wealthy nations will not be able to provide for them adequately.

Therefore, it is necessary, as in all things, to simplify your life, to conserve your resources and to begin to take the steps that you must take to regain your strength, to regain your focus, to assume your responsibilities and to provide for others effectively and wisely in the face of great change.

As it has been said, there may be other people you will have to take care of as well. For many segments of the population, even in wealthy nations, will be extremely vulnerable—the elderly, the infirm, children without parents or children with only one parent. If you are able, you must be in a position to assist them. For everyone will be poorer in the future as the Great Waves diminish the resources available to humanity and as economies begin the great and difficult adjustment to living in a world in decline.

Your economic reality will not be based upon growth but upon preservation. That will be a very different reality for most people. It is coming. You can see it. You can feel it. It does not require a genius to recognize this, only courage and sobriety.

Therefore, the financial well-being of your family, your family's health, your relationship with one another—all must be strengthened now. You must band together and work as a unit as much as possible. Your children will respond if they recognize there is great financial pressure now. Their play and their activities should be simple and natural. In the future, they may not have the technological pleasures or resources that they now might enjoy in a wealthy nation. They will have to adapt to this. Everyone will have to adapt—not just the poor, not just those who are facing misfortune, but everyone.

Your economic reality will not be based upon growth but upon preservation. That will be a very different reality for most people.

Here it may well be necessary for families to become united with each other to provide resources and assistance—networks of families, through civic organizations, through churches and so forth. The further ahead you plan for this, the better the position will be for you and for your family.

You may well have to deal with disagreement or disbelief. Unfortunately, humanity at its overall stage of evolution is not yet very intelligent. Intelligence here is the willingness and ability to learn and to adapt. This requires the willingness and ability to change as circumstances require it and to look ahead and to foresee the need for change. In this regard, humanity overall has not yet demonstrated its greater intelligence.

So you can expect that there will be disbelief and resistance. You can expect that many people will be critical. They will think that your approach and your ideas are too extreme and that what you are pointing to in the future is too radical, even impossible. But you cannot be dissuaded by this, for what is coming *is* a radical change, and that requires what will seem to many a radical preparation.

You must always have an adequate supply of food for your family, as much as you can store, for there will be times when food will become difficult to get or to purchase, and it will most certainly become ever more expensive.

You must practice great tolerance with your family, for they will all experience over time the strains of adjustment. It will be difficult for everyone. It will be difficult for your older children, who perhaps are used to living with a certain degree of affluence, to face a life without this affluence. Be very tolerant then with one another. Be as compassionate as you can. Be patient. But persevere. You must have a determined approach. You cannot let yourself fall behind in your preparation.

You must practice great tolerance with your family, for they will all experience over time the strains of adjustment.

If you have a family, it means you will have to become a leader of that family. It means you will have to take responsibility for setting a direction, taking steps and requiring others to go with you. It will be difficult, but it will also make you strong. Adversity will make you strong. Disagreement will make you strong. Ridicule will force you to trust yourself and to trust Knowledge within yourself.

Do not act out of fear or panic, for this leads to bad judgment. The state of mind that you want to achieve is one of clarity, objectivity and determination. You will go through periods of great anxiety and great fearfulness. You will go through periods, perhaps, when you will want to deny this reality, run away from it or find some more comfortable way to approach it or to consider it. You will want to lessen it and think that it is really not so bad and that you are overreacting

The state of mind that you want to achieve is one of clarity, objectivity and determination. to it. You will think that you should be more reasonable, more rational, which in reality means that you should act like other people act. You will have times when you will feel helpless and hopeless. Why prepare at all when it is so terrible?

Yet these are all emotional reactions. It is normal to have these kinds of reactions as long as they are not long lasting. It is part of the psychological adjustment to living in a declining world—a world of declining resources, a world of declining opportunities and a world of greater stress—requiring greater cohesion and unity between peoples.

It is a strange reality that the more affluent people are, the more separated they are. The more wealth people have, the further they seek to be from one another, the more isolated they become and the more they focus on their relationship with things rather than with each other. This wealth that is sought so feverishly and so compulsively actually weakens the human family and destroys individuals who claim to be its beneficiaries.

In the future, people will have to unite together. There will have to be greater cooperation. There will have to be greater restraints on what people can do, just to make cities and communities function. You will have fewer personal freedoms in the future, and that will be difficult. Out of necessity, people will have to follow certain courses of action within communities as resources diminish and as the need to care for people, particularly those who are most vulnerable, becomes ever more paramount. Lawlessness and crime will increase, and this will be a great difficulty.

These are things that perhaps you have felt already, or perhaps they are things you have not thought of at all. But when you begin to look over the horizon and see the signs of the world, and as you gain a greater objectivity—moving beyond the paroxysmal response of hope and fear to a place of greater objectivity—you will be able to see the picture, the possibilities and the difficulties that are certain to arise. You will see how people will respond to the requirements of great change. You will see people fight, struggle and compete. You will see people in denial. You will see people blaming others, blaming governments and blaming God. You will see violence. You will see tragedy. But you will also see great human courage and great human integrity.

The difficult times ahead have the promise of bringing people into a greater functioning unity than they have ever enjoyed before. Only in times of war have certain nations united together with such determination. Now you are fighting against the product of humanity's misuse of the world. Now you will be fighting against the consequences of human greed, ignorance and conflict. And now you will have to contend with intervention from predatory races in the Universe who are here to take advantage of a weak and divided humanity.

The difficult times ahead have the promise of bringing people into a greater functioning unity than they have ever enjoyed before.

It is like entering a great war, but it is not a war against other people. It is a war against circumstances. It is a war against the product of humanity's long and unhappy past. It is a struggle against nature, in a sense, in that you now must deal with the reality of living in a declining world, where ever greater numbers of people will be drinking from a slowly shrinking well.

The great threshold here is facing the great threshold—for yourself, for your family, for your spouse or partner, for your community and for all the other people whom you care about.

You now must deal with the reality of living in a declining world, where ever greater numbers of people will be drinking from a slowly shrinking well.

That is why the inner preparation is so vitally necessary. If you panic, you will do foolish things and make very unwise and even tragic decisions. If you try to tell everyone at once what you are seeing, you will be overwhelmed with discouragement. Instead, in quiet, before you proclaim anything beyond your family, you must build your inner strength.

It is as if you are facing a great mountain, and you must climb this mountain. You must gather together what you need, the provisions that you will need, leaving aside anything that is unnecessary for the journey. You brace yourself for making this climb—building your physical strength, your mental strength, resolving as much as you can, simplifying your life, simplifying your range of concern and focusing your mind and attention.

You will see, as time progresses, the tragedy of people being swept away, losing everything in the Great Waves of change. As economic instability grows, people will be losing their jobs, their careers and their homes. It is already happening in so many places. You will see more social disorder, particularly in large and expanding cities, but also in rural areas as local economies begin to collapse.

You will see these things, and if you are unprepared, they will be overwhelming to you, and there will be little you can do eventually to prepare for them. That is why this time is so important to see what others cannot see, to feel what others will not feel and to do what others will not do. This gives you the greatest advantage and will require great strength from you. You will need this strength as never before.

Therefore, do not complain. Do not reject these words. Do not try to fall back into a comfortable state of mind with all your comfortable conclusions and assumptions. Do not retreat into some earlier or past experience. Do not look for an escape, to escape to some place or situation where you will not have to deal with these things, for such places will not exist now.

From a higher vantage point and from a greater wisdom, the Great Waves of change are what humanity has created for itself to force a kind of redemption. Unable to use its affluence effectively, it must now use its failure. Humanity must now use adversity to redeem itself. This redemption is not guaranteed, but under more dire circumstances, people do show the ability to unite together in a more selfless manner. People do have the ability to unite to save one another. It is like being in a house on fire. Everyone must pitch in or the house is lost. Everyone must participate or people are lost. It is like being on a ship that is slowly sinking. Everyone is forced into action to save the vessel and to save not only themselves, but to save everyone.

The Great Waves of change will require this kind of selfless action increasingly, and for those who can cultivate this selfless approach to life, they will be in a position to lead others, to help others, to rescue others and to empower others. Those who are worshipped and idolized today may be replaced by a whole different set of leaders whose skills and whose compassion raise them above everyone else. Those who are glamorous, those who are famous, those who are beautiful, those who are charming—what will they offer to a world in decline? Their chances are no better than the average person and in some cases much worse.

This time is so important to see what others cannot see, to feel what others will not feel and to do what others will not do.

This will require a different kind of strength from people— a core strength, the strength of Knowledge. This will require greater integrity, greater wisdom and greater cooperation—the real merits and the real abilities of the human family. In affluence, people are dissolute, but in adversity, people can do magnificent things.

Just taking care of your family, becoming a leader in your family, setting the vision, taking the steps and being unwilling to give up your responsibilities because of the desires or preferences of others—this represents a greatness in you. Do not shrink from this or you will shrink from the very circumstances that you have come into the world to serve, and you will put your family in jeopardy as a result.

You cannot save humanity. You cannot save the world. You cannot save your nation. You cannot save your city or your town. But you must save those who are close to you, and you must save those amongst your neighbors who are most vulnerable and who will be most greatly endangered by the circumstances to come.

In affluence, people are dissolute, but in adversity, people can do magnificent things.

There will have to be much sharing and much cooperation. There will have to be much public service. There will have to be a great restraint of violence and self-destructive behavior. The circumstances will require this. Many people will be at great risk—the very old, the very young, the disabled and the handicapped. Many people will have to step forward to give more than they are accustomed to giving. Their time and their energy will now be devoted to caring for others. This will be a requirement. Everyone will need to pitch in, or whole cities and communities could collapse into chaos and terrible violence. Starvation could occur even in the wealthiest places as food distribution is disrupted.

The situation is terrible, horrible or redemptive, depending on how you look at it, depending on which state of mind you are functioning from. If you are functioning from your personal mind, then everything will look terrible, and you will want to deny it and dismiss it. If you cannot dismiss it, you will want to blame others for it and try to run away and find someplace to hide. However, from the greater state of mind of Knowledge, you recognize that the Great Waves were coming all along, that you have a role to play and that you must become very strong now, very compassionate and very forgiving.

That is why taking the steps to Knowledge is so important. It will secure your well-being and the well-being of your family and others whom you care for. Knowledge is not merely to have a high spiritual experience. Your very survival will depend upon it now, and your ability to be of service to others, for the needs of people will be far greater in the near future than they are today.

Your spirituality will be about caring for people, feeding people, serving people and taking care of the world around you. That will be your gift to God. That will be your service in the world. That will be what will reunite you with Knowledge within yourself and make you whole and complete.

The very circumstances that people deny, reject, avoid and are terrified of are the very circumstances that could redeem them, that could unite them within themselves and that could make them powerful and whole, effective and fulfilled.

If humanity cannot learn from its successes, then it must learn from its failures. If humanity cannot unite in its wealth, then it must unite in the loss of its wealth. For in a world of decline, wealth will be lost. Ultimately, wealth is tied to resources in the

Your spirituality will be about caring for people, feeding people, serving people and taking care of the world around you. That will be your gift to God.

If humanity cannot unite in its wealth, then it must unite in the loss of its wealth.

world. As resources decline, wealth will decline. A few may hold onto great wealth, but they will be extremely vulnerable as others turn against them. Where will they run and hide? They will live like slaves, like prisoners. They will be unable to go out in public, unable to show their faces, surrounded by guards. That will be their tragedy.

This is the world you have come to serve. Gain the strength beyond fear and preference. Gain the greater strength of Knowledge, which is clear, objective and compassionate. Become a student of Knowledge. Receive God's blessing and God's preparation. Look ahead, not trying to understand everything or to resolve everything, but to take the steps you must take.

You do not get to see the pathway and then decide if you want to take the journey. You must take the journey to see the pathway.

Ask yourself, "What must I do now in order to prepare myself and my family?" Already there are things you know you must do. Perhaps you have known them for some time. You must do them now. Do the things you know you must do today, and tomorrow you will know other things that you must do. If you do them, you will know more things that you must do. It is by doing that you gain greater clarity. Completing the tasks you know you must do shows you the other tasks that must be completed.

The pathway opens up before you. You cannot hold yourself back and see it all. There is no guarantee of success in life. There is no assurance that everything you do will work out perfectly. You do not get to see the pathway and then decide if you want to take the journey. You must take the journey to see the pathway.

Knowledge within you knows what must be done. It knows how to respond to the world far beyond what your intellect is capable of. Yet even your intellect will have to be brought into great service here—working together with Knowledge, uniting you within yourself, bringing all of your assets and your gained wisdom to bear.

To know what to do beyond what you are doing now, you will have to complete what you are doing now, and then the next steps will appear. This is how the journey is revealed. And this is the journey that you must take.

CHAPTER 8

The Danger of Isolation

In the face of the Great Waves of change, it is important that you are not isolated and that other people know who you are and where you are—people who can assist you, people whose wisdom you can rely upon, people who can support you in times of need. This network of relationships, to whatever extent it can be established or is established already, is vitally important.

You will need great assistance from others. You will not be able to completely take care of yourself in the face of the Great Waves of change. You will need others for guidance, for assistance, and, under great duress, you will need someone to help you to feed yourself and take care of yourself. It will be a great dilemma for those who are isolated, for those who have never built a functioning and supportive network of relationships.

It is unwise to live far away from the cities, where provisions can be provided and where you can gain access to the very fundamental things that you will need. If you are far away from the cities and are not closely engaged with your neighbors, you will be isolated and on your own.

In the future, people will be abandoning their homes in the distant country, seeking food, energy, shelter and security. It will not be safe living alone in outlying districts, as there will be much crime and thievery. This will be due to the fact that there will be many people out of work, desperately seeking for anything that they can use or sell. For someone living alone in

In the future, people will be abandoning their homes in the distant country, seeking food, energy, shelter and security.

the country, they will be very vulnerable, and law enforcement will not be sufficient to protect them, for the needs of rural communities will be so immense that law enforcement will be overwhelmed.

That is why your preparation for the Great Waves must begin far in advance of extreme or difficult situations. If you wait, if you hold yourself back from your preparation, if you wait until there is agreement and consensus, then you will have very few options. You will have very few options and very few choices. Here, as has been the case throughout human history, your strength will lie in Knowledge within you and within your primary relationships and community, to whatever extent they have been established.

That is why now is the time to begin to share the reality of the Great Waves with those people whom you know—with your friends and your relatives, even with your neighbors. Perhaps only a few of them will be able to respond, but nonetheless you are building your own social security for the future, for there will be very little social security from your governments.

Your situation then has to be completely reevaluated, and that is part of the deep evaluation that will be required. You will have to figure out how to find a way to get to your neighbors, your friends and your allies, particularly if you live in a rural area where the distances can be great. Rural living will become very hazardous unless you have established a high degree of self-sufficiency. But that is very difficult to achieve and can only be prolonged for a certain period of time.

In the future, agricultural areas will be protected to some degree, but many people live in rural areas who are not focused primarily on agriculture, thinking they want to be closer to nature as in an early era. Thinking they want to be away from the stress and the difficulties of living in cities and urban areas, they move now far away.

But the world is changing. Your situation is changing and will change even more. What you previously sought as a reprieve, as a retreat, now becomes a hazard. When fuel supplies become extremely low and there are shortages, how will you function? Even your nearest towns may not have food, petroleum and medicine, for these things will be focused in large cities, where large congregations of people live. Outlying districts will have difficulty acquiring even the most fundamental things.

Everything has to be reconsidered in the face of the Great Waves of change. Isolation here, even within a large city, is very hazardous. And this is particularly true for single mothers. It is particularly true for the elderly. It is particularly true for children and for people who have handicaps and are disabled. How will they know what to do when there are shortages of food, or shortages of water, or shortages of petroleum, or when they are unable to heat their homes or their apartments? For all these circumstances will arise within the Great Waves of change, even in the wealthy nations.

Do not think here that if you live in a rural area that you can stockpile food and medicine, for how long will that last you? And what will prevent people coming to steal it from you, coming in the night, coming in the day? Your retreat has now become an isolation, a hazardous isolation.

In the future, people will flock to the cities for food, for energy, for medicine and for security. Great congregations of people will come from outlying districts, where supplies will fall short. You do not want to be at the bottom of the list, living in a town or a village. It could

What you previously sought as a reprieve, as a retreat, now becomes a hazard.

take weeks or months for supplies to reach you.

People think, "Oh, this cannot be. It is impossible. This will never happen!" But this has happened countless times throughout human history, and in the face of the Great Waves of change, these circumstances are inevitable. How is your nation going to survive and function on half of the energy resources it is using now? And who will be the first to receive these resources and to receive assistance from your government?

It is a different world you are entering, a different set of circumstances. If you can see the Great Waves of change—if you will take the time to study them, to read about them and to consider them—you will see how absolutely vulnerable you are and how vulnerable people are who are isolated—geographically isolated, socially isolated or circumstantially isolated.

How is your nation going to survive and function on half of the energy resources it is using now?

That is why it is so important to educate your friends, family and neighbors about the Great Waves of change, to collaborate with them and to create a plan of assistance—to have contingency plans in case certain things transpire, to have homes where you can gather, to build a reserve of resources so that you are not immediately in danger and to bond together if necessary and provide assistance and support for one another.

This community preparedness is so vitally important, even in outlying rural areas. You will have to have enough provisions to provide for yourself in the interim, to support people who may come to you who have nothing, to consider the predicament for elderly persons living in your proximity and to have enough resources to provide for them if necessary or to assist them. This will make the difference between a set of circumstances being difficult and being catastrophic.

Community preparedness is very important. It is very significant. That is why this book has provided "Recommendations" for preparing for the Great Waves of change. These are beginning steps. If people will take these steps, they will be in a much better position. But to change one's circumstances takes time and takes effort and courage and is often quite difficult to do, particularly if you are in a family where others do not agree with you.

Time is of the essence then. You need this time to consider where you live, how you live, how you can get about, where you will be able to provision yourself, where those provisions might be and to build a network of support with your friends, family and neighbors who are living in your proximity. This will give you time to relieve yourself of unnecessary possessions, activities or obligations that are draining your energy away from this primary focus and emphasis.

If there are shortages of fuel, what will you do? This is a particularly serious problem for people living in outlying rural areas or far away from distribution centers. They will be the last to receive whatever provisions can be provided. How are they going to function in their homes, on their farms and in their personal retreats? And how long will they be able to last, even if they have set aside resources and provisions? Even the "Recommendations" given in this book emphasize that stockpiling resources and provisions is only a short-term emphasis. It is only to enable you to pass through shocks or difficult periods. They are not permanent solutions.

It is very important, then, that you begin to face the Great Waves of change and to share this message with others and to honestly discuss with them, if they are open to it, ways that you can be of future

Time is of the essence then. You need this time to consider where you live, how you live, how you can get about.

The wise are always considering what is coming over the horizon. They are always looking and watching.

assistance to one another if necessary.

As you can see through reading the words in this book what a great and significant thing this really is, how quickly people's circumstances can change, how little it would take to throw your situation into enormous jeopardy and how utterly reliant you are upon resources coming from afar—resources that you take for granted, resources that you never question. What would happen if they were no longer available to you?

You must think of these things now—not emotionally, but reasonably—considering your advantages and disadvantages based upon where you live, how you live and how you travel about. What assets do you have? What are your liabilities? What is the strength of your position? Do you need to change your living circumstances radically in the face of the Great Waves of change? If so, you will need to do this fairly quickly because these things take time, and time is what you do not have a lot of. If there are shortages of fuel, or if the price of everything escalates beyond what you can afford, what will you do then? Complain? Cry? Break down? Have a tantrum? Having never thought of these things before, the shock will be overwhelming to you, and you will have few choices in what to do.

That is why the wise are always considering what is coming over the horizon. They are always looking and watching. They are not afraid and not terrified, but cautious. For all the people who are sensing great change in the world, and there are many of you who are experiencing this even now, it is important to look at what that change might be and how you will need to prepare yourself for it, given whatever resources that you have.

Here you cannot rely upon governments or political parties or technological innovations, for these alone will not be sufficient to protect the people—the people of your nation, the people of your city, the people of your town or village—from the great impacts of the Great Waves of change.

Because the climate will be changing, there will be a tremendous loss of food productivity in the world. And because fuel supplies will become more expensive and difficult to get, it will be harder for large farms to produce enough food. Food will be a major emphasis, as it is already in the poorer nations. But even in the wealthy nations, food will be a major priority— not simply the price of food, but the availability of food. That is why you maintain a provision to last you at least a month so you have time to consider what you must do next and not simply be thrown into panic or desperation.

If you can begin to prepare, you will gain confidence. If you do nothing, you will lose heart. You will be defeated before the trials have even appeared, before the difficulties have even really reached you. Some people will capitulate even at the idea that they must reconsider their lives and prepare for the Great Waves of change. It is sad that their courage and integrity have become so weakened that they would give in so easily. Their plight will be extreme. Now it will be up to other people to take care of them, when in fact it is they who should be taking care of other people.

You will see this. You will see all the demonstrations of human ignorance, human denial, human folly and human fantasy in the face of the Great Waves of change. Everything will become amplified. If someone was being foolish before, they will likely be more foolish now. If someone was living on a set of weak assumptions, they will assert those assumptions even more strongly now. If someone was living in a state of denial, they will increase their expression of denial until they can no longer do so.

> *If you can begin to prepare, you will gain confidence. If you do nothing, you will lose heart.*

Here you must be prepared. There will be utter panic, chaos and desperation around you as people, now caught off guard, have to face a really difficult situation for which they have not prepared—a situation that is now undermining their whole life and reality.

What would it take to produce such a powerful impact? A fuel shortage in your nation, your state or your region—that alone would do it. A violent weather event. A hurricane, a tornado or extreme drought as the planet heats, and all of a sudden, there is not enough water for both human beings and for agriculture. It would take so very little to throw your life into jeopardy.

Everyone is living on a set of assumptions based upon a weak and fragile infrastructure. Should the infrastructure break, as it will, people will suddenly be thrown into desperation and confusion. It is those who can be forewarned, it is those who have the courage to face the inevitable changes that will come and the grave possibilities they bring with them that will be strong enough to withstand these challenges and to provide strength, encouragement and direction for others.

Everyone is living on a set of assumptions based upon a weak and fragile infrastructure.

Therefore, do not worry about trying to change the awareness of everyone. It is your awareness that must change. It is you who must reach out to whoever is in your proximity that can support and assist you in your efforts. People have talents. They have wisdom. They have skills. These will all have to be brought together for the welfare of everyone involved. Even if you cannot get your town or city to develop a preparation plan, you can still reach out to certain people and establish a network with them.

The situation calls for human strength, but it will also reveal human weakness in all of its manifestations. A great difficulty the human family has is in not preparing for the future—not preparing for the real future, not thinking ahead, not being able to look out on the world with clear and objective eyes and not considering the possibilities, the probabilities and the extreme likelihood of great change.

You are living in a world of decline. The availability of fuel, the availability of electricity, the availability of food, and in some places water, will become ever greater problems as your environment is unable to provide for the over-arching demands of people and the way that they live.

Medicines will be difficult to acquire, particularly if you are living in outlying or rural regions. It will not be as it is today, where you can simply order things electronically and they will be delivered. Such deliveries may not be possible in the future. What are you going to do if you require these medications?

These are all extremely practical and realistic questions now. Perhaps they were unthinkable before, and you never concerned yourself with them. But now you must concern yourself with them, for you are facing a set of changes in the world that will alter the availability and the distribution of resources, fundamental resources. And you will see how vulnerable you really are in even considering these things, particularly if you are living in isolation geographically or socially. That is why it takes time to build access to other people who are aware of the Great Waves of change, to help one another to consider what must be done and to use the "Recommendations" that are presented here as a starting point.

It will require a lot of energy and time to do this—energy and time that now is being given to things of perhaps little or no value, or things that are certainly not

You are facing a set of changes in the world that will alter the availability and the distribution of resources, fundamental resources.

essential for your future well-being. Take all of the energy that you might use currently in complaining about the world, complaining about other people, complaining about your government or complaining about life, and bring that focus and energy to bear in preparing for the Great Waves of change, in building a network of support with other people and in educating your local community. The majority of people are unaware that the Great Waves are coming, and when those Waves arrive, they will not be ready.

Life is about living fully in the moment and about preparing wisely for the future. That is what the animals do. That is what human beings must learn to do if they are to be intelligent. It is coming back into the natural world and leaving your artificial world of technology—your artificial world that is based upon weak assumptions, assumptions based upon a weak and overextended infrastructure—that supports you with what you need.

Do not think that because the nation you live in is large and highly populated and that there is wealth and technology that it cannot fail in the face of the Great Waves of change and that society itself cannot be undone at the very core. Even as food becomes more expensive, and in places unavailable, it is going to push your economic stability over the edge. And this is happening already. Think now, what would happen if this price increase did not stop?

> *Life is about living fully in the moment and about preparing wisely for the future.*

You are preparing for a world in decline. If you have lived in a wealthy and affluent nation, it is going to be a very difficult recognition and transition to make. It will be difficult in large part because of your ideas, your assumptions and your beliefs and the weakness that has been established over time in disabling you from facing difficult and unexpected circumstances.

Therefore, you must bridge your isolation. Become involved in your local community. Speak in your local city councils and governments. Find out what your town or your city or your nation is doing to prepare for these great difficulties. Read, become educated, go visit people, participate. Escape your isolation and self-obsession. Become involved. Become an advocate. Share the revelation in this book with other people. Read what other people are discovering as they begin to discern the Great Waves of change. This is healthy for you. It is redemptive for you. It will give you confidence if you act. If you do nothing, your confidence will fall away, and you will sink into despair. Then you will be truly powerless and truly vulnerable.

If you live in a desert region, you may have to leave, as there may be no water for you in the future.

The situation calls for you to become powerful, for you to become engaged with others, for you to escape your own hellish isolation, for you to take action, for you to realize your strength, to utilize your skills and to utilize the skills of other people, knowing that alone you cannot prepare adequately for the great change that is coming now.

If you live in a desert region, you may have to leave, as there may be no water for you in the future, and it may be very difficult for food to reach your community. Do not live near moving water, near rivers that will overflow in the face of violent weather and changing climate conditions. It is wise to move away from coastal regions that will be affected by violent weather and in many cases from certain large cities that will be subject to extreme social unrest.

Knowledge within you, the greater intelligence that God has given you, will give you direction and will give you signs and will provide steps for you to take. You take these steps without fully understanding the whole process or the outcome. You

You first must build your ark. And you must build the ark before the rains come, before the great change is upon you.

simply take the steps. Knowledge will speak to you through your thoughts, through your feelings. But it will not speak through fear, it will not speak through fantasy, and it will not speak to your preferences. You must be open, asking Knowledge within yourself, "What must I do now? What is the next step for me? How shall I regard this particular situation? What decision should I make regarding this particular thing?"

You must stay with this. You have to get past fear and rejection, shock and awe, to get into a place of greater clarity and objectivity so that you can respond to Knowledge, feel Knowledge, hear Knowledge and see the signs that Knowledge is giving you.

You cannot solve this problem for the world. You cannot solve this problem for the nation. You first must build your ark. And you must build the ark before the rains come, before the great change is upon you. You must help others build arks, and you must join your ark with theirs so that you have relationship and community.

Your strength is in Knowledge, relationship and community. All three of these now become primary. It is more important than wealth. It is more important than pleasure. It is more important than seeking escape. It is more important than your hobbies and your obsessions. It is more important than your romances and your tragedies. Building your connection to Knowledge, building strong relationships with others and becoming part of a community of preparation—this is what really matters.

You must function on only partial awareness and partial certainty. You will not know everything that needs to be done. No one knows that. You will have to choose carefully who you listen to, for some people will give you very bad advice. Even people who are aware of the Great Waves of change can give you very bad advice as to what you must do.

Here the strength of your relationships will help you, for it is more difficult to deceive two minds than it is to deceive one. Here you must bring everything to Knowledge. Ask Knowledge, "Is this a good idea?" Ask Knowledge, "Should I follow the recommendations of this person?" Perhaps you will feel resistance; perhaps Knowledge will be silent. Both indicate that you should stop and not proceed with that decision or follow that person.

You must be patient. You must be observant. If you are frightened and panicked, you will do extreme and unwise things. You have to face great danger with courage and with as much objectivity as you can muster. This requires the power of Knowledge within yourself. And it requires the confidence that you can take action, that you can move your life in a positive direction and that you will not fall into the trap of easy assumptions or simple solutions, thinking you have an answer for everything.

Do not underestimate the risks and the power of the Great Waves. Many people will do this, thinking, "Oh, well, you just provide this new technology, and it's not a problem" or "You just have people change their behavior in this one way, and everything is fine." Others will say, "It is not really a big problem. It is all being invented by other people for their own profit or advantages." You will hear a whole range of responses to the Great Waves of change. But only within yourself, in the depth of your experience, will you know, and if you listen carefully, you will see who amongst others is wise and who is unwise.

One should never underestimate adversity when entering into changing circumstances. That is basic wisdom

Your strength is in Knowledge, relationship and community.

One should never underestimate adversity when entering into changing circumstances. regarding living in physical reality. Many people do this, of course. Some people do this in facing anything and everything. But for you, you must gain a greater strength, a greater confidence and with it a greater patience. You have to follow the steps. You cannot simply have big answers. Big answers will not be true answers. Everything has to be tried and proven. You do not climb a great mountain in one giant leap. You have to prepare yourself and your provisions, and you have to take the long journey and build strength and wisdom as you go.

Do not worry that others are not doing this. Do not worry that the general population seems asleep and falsely self-assured. You yourself must prepare. Against all odds, you must prepare. Against the discouragement you will see in observing others, you must still prepare. You prepare because you must— not because everyone is doing it, not because the experts have told you that you must do it. Even most of the experts do not know what is coming and are not responding appropriately.

You are being given a gift of love here. If you can appreciate the problem, you will see the value of the answer. If you can recognize the great challenge coming now, you will appreciate the gift of preparation. You will not see it as an inconvenience. You will not think of it in a negative way. You will not deny it, repudiate it or think it is too extreme. In fact, it is quite appropriate in the face of the Great Waves.

This preparation will redeem you. It will free you from your own self-obsession, your own weaknesses, your own foolishness and your own preoccupations. It will require you to respond to life and to the world and to reality. You will find you have strength you did not know you had before. If you take action, you will realize that you have this strength and can build this strength. If you reach out to others, you will find that others have strength and you will need their strength as well, as they will need yours.

This will be life affirming, for people were meant to function together in harmony. People do not do well when they are living in isolation, whether it be geographical isolation, social isolation or psychological isolation. People wither and shrink in isolation, but become stronger in functioning together for a greater purpose. Now you have a greater purpose. You do not have to wonder now, "Who am I, why am I in the world, and what am I really here to do?" because life is telling you what you must do, and Knowledge within you is urging you to respond. You are freed from endless deliberation, self-questioning, self-evaluation and self-obsession, for now you must respond to the world.

You yourself must prepare. Against all odds, you must prepare. Against the discouragement you will see in observing others, you must still prepare.

It will take time to gain certain information that you will need, but it must lead to wise and constructive action. You must prepare before the Great Waves come. You must prepare before others realize what is happening. You are being given this early warning. It is a blessing of unparalleled value and importance for you.

Rethink your life—your relationship with where you live, the house you live in, your work, your transportation, your relationships. Who is wise amongst those whom you know? Who has skills? Who is strong? Who can face the Great Waves of change? Learn what the resources of your community are. What can they provide? What assets do they really have that can support you and your community?

The work is immense. It is necessary. And now is the time. There is no more time for just foolish consideration, thinking about the problem. And it is not appropriate to simply be frightened and do nothing. If you act, you will become stronger and more confident. If you do not act, you will become weaker and less confident. Action is necessary. There is so much to do, and now is the time to take this action.

It is as if your nation were going to enter a great war that will decide the fate of the world. You must think of the Great Waves like this, except now you are going to be at war with the world, with the conditions of the world that have largely been created by humanity's overuse and abuse of the world's resources and environment. It is going to war with the circumstances you have created, circumstances that can now defeat you and overwhelm you.

Now you have a greater purpose. You do not have to wonder now, "Who am I, why am I in the world, and what am I really here to do?"

You must think of it in a big way, or you will diminish it because you are afraid. You will diminish it because you are not confident. You will diminish it because everyone else is diminishing the risk. You will fall back into complacency and false self-assurance, re-engaging with your former interests and priorities. You were awake for a few minutes. You were alerted, but then you fell back into a state of slumber—sleeping now, unaware, unprepared and assured that everything will be taken care of for you by someone, somewhere, somehow.

This is the weakness of humanity. It has lost its strength, its awareness and its response to nature—living in insulation, living in affluence, living on self-assurance. The wealth and splendor that were created in the last century will diminish and decline in this century—decline rapidly, as if a great balloon were deflating, so vulnerable it was from being punctured by so many things.

You must adjust and adapt. That is being intelligent. To deny this is not being intelligent. Living in isolation is not intelligent. There are very few people who will be able to survive in isolation, but they will have to have immense skills and will have to live a life of continued hardship. This would only work for a very, very unique set of individuals. For everyone else, which is nearly everyone else, there will have to be greater human cooperation and a very careful use of resources.

The whole human landscape will have to be redesigned over time so that people can function and live under a very different set of circumstances in a world in decline. In the future, whole cities will be abandoned due to the heating of the world. If you live in a city like this now, you must consider relocation. Whole regions of the world will become so arid that almost no one will be able to live there. They will have to move. Where should they go? What should they do? And who would receive them?

You cannot answer these questions. You do not have an answer for these questions. But you have a journey to take. You have a preparation to make. You have a pathway to follow. You were always meant to have this preparation, this journey and this pathway. Now is the time that you must begin and proceed. You cannot control the outcome for the world, but you can build greater stability for yourself and for other people, and this is important. This is within the realm of your responsibility and capability, and this is what you must do now.

CHAPTER 9

The Great Waves Prophecy

THE QUESTION WILL SURELY ARISE: What can you expect
regarding the Great Waves of change?

Specifically, what will take place will be determined in part
by humanity's ability to respond and to prepare. What will take
place is that the world will become warmer, producing greater
loss of food production and great scarcity of water resources in
many places in the world while there will be tremendous
flooding in other places. Energy resources will diminish,
creating economic upheaval and in some places even collapse.

Everything will become immensely expensive. There will be
great competition and a great risk of conflict and war over
gaining access to the remaining resources. Certain regions will
be devastated. Others will be impaired. Many industries will
fail. There will be many people out of work.

There will be the risk of great starvation in many parts of
the world, even in parts of the wealthy nations. There will have
to be ever-increasing international agreements. Food will have
to be distributed where it is needed most. There will be great
shortages of medicine and medical care, even in the wealthy
nations. There will be tremendously destructive weather events.

The risk of war itself will produce conflict on a scale never
seen before in this world. If this conflict can be prevented or
minimized, it will make an immense difference in the outcome
for humanity. But a certain degree of conflict will arise, particularly in the poorer nations, within them and between them.

There will be environmental refugees, and there will be war refugees on a scale never seen before.

And there is a great risk that other nations, now desperate for resources, will enter into conflict with one another.

Governments will have to become more controlling, minimizing human freedom, even in the freest nations. It will be an emergency that will continue. Many people will struggle against this. There will be much human tragedy and much human bravery and courage.

Large areas of the world that are now highly inhabited will become uninhabitable, as it will be impossible to grow food there due to lack of water. There will be immense migrations of people away from such areas and away from areas of conflict. There will be environmental refugees, and there will be war refugees on a scale never seen before.

There will be a great risk of pandemic illness that will arise out of deteriorating conditions, particularly in large urban areas. Many people may perish. It will be an immense and traumatic set of events.

Yet in the midst of this, there will be great human ingenuity. Technology must develop new pathways of providing energy to people, mostly through forms of electricity. There will have to be immense efficiency and the uniting of resources within nations and in many cases between nations.

Yet even the best human efforts will not prevent the massive change and disruptions that will occur. But human ingenuity and human cooperation will determine whether humanity will have a future and whether human civilization can survive and can build a new foundation of unity and cooperation.

Therefore, you cannot escape the Great Waves of change. But you can minimize their damaging effects, and you can benefit from them in many ways—setting a new course for humanity, building a stronger international community of people advancing technology, advancing social justice and advancing human welfare. But it will not be easy. It in fact will be the most difficult thing humanity has ever attempted. It will take great commitment, great courage, great faith, great cooperation and great personal restraint.

Even the best human efforts will not prevent the massive change and disruptions that will occur.

It will require a New Message from God to provide the clarity, wisdom and Knowledge that humanity will need now if it is to capitalize on its strengths and avoid capitulating to its weaknesses.

Travel will be extremely difficult, if not impossible. People will live locally, work locally and will have to survive locally. Local food production and local manufacturing will become ever more important. Everything will have to function on a smaller scale.

Those who have resources will have to share them by sending them abroad to starving peoples and to areas of the world that are in great crisis. The humanitarian effort will be immense, almost unimaginable by today's standards. Wealthier nations will have to receive the people who are escaping areas that have been devastated or where food production can no longer take place. The areas of the world where humanity will be able to live will shrink, forcing millions of people to move elsewhere and to resettle.

This is so different from the fantasies and the imagination of human societies today—building ever-grander cities, building ever-faster conveyances, building ever more remarkable personal conveniences and luxuries. Such

The humanitarian effort will be immense, almost unimaginable by today's standards.

Your visionaries are discarded, ignored or vilified while everyone continues to devastate the world, to deplete its resources and to diminish its future possibilities.

foolishness. So blind. So reckless. So ignorant and so unintelligent. These forces are pushing humanity further and further towards the edge of collapse, pushing humanity to overuse the world even more—heedless of the signs that many thresholds have already been passed.

Those who are visionary and who can see what is coming over the horizon are condemned as being negative, unspiritual or doomsday people. Your visionaries are discarded, ignored or vilified while everyone continues to devastate the world, to deplete its resources and to diminish its future possibilities.

While there are great sources of energy that humanity has not yet discovered, it is a long way from discovering them, and it will have to survive the Great Waves of change even to have a chance of discovering them.

The transition period to a new stability in the world will be long and very difficult. It is not impossible. In fact, it must happen. But do not think that it will happen in and of itself. Do not think that technology alone will make it possible.

The human population will have to become much smaller in the future, hopefully by human will and through compassionate means. If not, then nature will devastate the human population—nature, conflict and war.

You will have a smaller world to live in. Perhaps only a billion people could live here, maybe two, but not much more. That is with your advanced technology and your best efforts, a strong international community, tremendous cooperation and the mitigation and the limiting of conflict and war. In other words, if everything is done well and correctly, with immense human contribution, you will still have to have a small world population.

If these actions are not taken, if humanity will not and cannot prepare, if it cannot restrain its own greed, corruption and competition with one another, then the results will be far worse, so much worse that words cannot describe it—a collapse of civilization, an immense reduction of the human population, further devastating the world and depleting its resources.

And beyond this, you have the hidden threat of intervention and competition from the Greater Community, the Universe. There is already an Intervention in the world, positioning itself to assume the reins of power, to present itself as the savior of humanity and to establish its networks of support and its legion of human representatives. This Intervention is seeking to influence public opinion, to position itself as the noble saviors of humanity and in some cases even as the parents of humanity in order to weave its tentacles into the human fabric. The Intervention is creating a hybrid individual capable of advising and eventually leading the human family, an individual with no human allegiance whatsoever, an individual with no compassion, respect or empathy for humanity.

This is how foreign races that do not possess military assets can gain control of a large world full of violent individuals. These intervening races will support humanity's decline and will undermine the strength of the strongest nations, setting them in competition and conflict with one another. They will encourage human conflict by promising world dominance to certain leaders of nations and religions.

Humanity is easily misled. It is divided. It is superstitious. It is ignorant of life beyond the world, life in the Greater Community of worlds, life in the Universe.

All the Intervention needs is time for humanity to weaken itself to such a point that the Intervention

The transition period to a new stability in the world will be long and very difficult.

can present itself, either publicly or behind the scenes, to gain the reins of power. If that should take place, then humanity will have lost its greatest asset—its freedom and its self-determination.

You can see already how difficult it is to face these things and how weak you are in your inability to face them. You may be physically strong. Maybe you can run ten miles. Maybe you can assert yourself in your business affairs. Maybe you are very strong in your viewpoint, but emotionally and psychologically, you can see here how weak and incapable you can be—how much you may want to run away, how much you may insist upon solutions, how much you may go into denial, how easily you may fall into hopelessness and how much you may protest and rage against others, people and governments, unable to simply look and face the Great Waves of change.

If humanity cannot advance in times of success, it must advance in times of failure.

You must face this. If you cannot, you will run away, your preparation will not happen and you will be ever more vulnerable to the power of all of these great events.

The New Message is here to prepare you, but to prepare you, it first must warn you. If you do not see the gravity of the problem, you will not recognize the significance of the solution. If you do not see that you really do not have an answer for all of these things, then you will not be in a position to accept the grace and the power that God is providing the world. If you will not accept the reality, then you will not recognize the remedy.

The situation is far more serious than you realize and will require from you a greater strength than you think you have, but which in reality you do have. Your faith in yourself, your faith in people, your faith in nations and your faith in the power of Knowledge within you and within others will have to be so much stronger than it is today. You will have to let go of your judgments, your hatred, your prejudices, your cynicism, your jaded perspectives, your foolish hopes and wishes and your fantasies.

Yet to release these things is to be renewed to a real power and your ability to enjoy life in the moment and to prepare for life in the future. It is to renew your ability to be with others, to be with yourself, to enjoy all the real benefits of life and the promise of realizing and fulfilling your greater purpose here.

You do not yet see that to prepare for the Great Waves of change is the pathway that will redeem you to yourself and to God. This will make you strong, compassionate, competent and wise—wiser than you are today. It will give you an escape from your unhappy past and unfortunate circumstances to a new life—a life of purpose, meaning and contribution.

If humanity cannot advance in times of success, it must advance in times of failure. If humanity cannot unite and build its core strength together in times of abundance and affluence, it must do so in times of diminishing opportunities and diminishing resources.

There are three things that humanity must achieve in order to be a free race within a Greater Community of intelligent life. It must be united. It must be self-sufficient. And it must be extremely discreet. It must be united in the sense that it is functioning together as a whole. It is not that everyone loves each other, gets along or sees things in the same way, but humanity must function together as a complete unit.

Humanity's self-sufficiency means that everything you need comes from this one world so that you are not dependent upon trade and influence with others in the Greater Community— others who would easily take advantage of a young, emerging race such as your own.

And you must be extremely discreet, which means you are not broadcasting all of your communications out into space, revealing to anyone who cares to look everything you think,

You are heading towards a position of extreme powerlessness and vulnerability in the Universe.

everything you do, your weaknesses, your strengths, your secrets—everything.

Clearly, you can see humanity's great vulnerability in the Universe. You are not united. You are still engaged in tribal, sectarian warfare, in competition and conflict, rapidly destroying the world's resources in doing so. Your self-sufficiency is being lost with every passing day as you squander and diminish your natural inheritance here in the world—diminishing your most vital and fundamental resources, driving the world towards the Great Waves of change. And you are hardly discreet as you are projecting nearly everything out into space through your radio transmissions.

You do not realize your immense vulnerability here. For in the Universe, the strong will dominate the weak if they can, as it is here on Earth. Nature does not change with technology. Everyone in the Universe is searching for resources, and those advanced races who have outstripped their own worlds' resources must now trade and search for these resources wherever they can. The competition and the deception around this are immense, beyond anything you can possibly imagine. It is simply nature happening on a much grander scale.

If humanity were well versed in the affairs of life in your local Universe, you would be ending war *today*. You would be preserving resources *today*. You would be rationing energy *today*. You would be preserving your environment *today*. You would be maintaining biological diversity *today*. You would be confining your communications through other media *today*. And yesterday.

You are heading towards a position of extreme powerlessness and vulnerability in the Universe, and because you live in a world of such immense biological diversity and wealth, you do not realize its importance to others. You are like the native tribe living in the jungle, isolated from the rest of the world, living in a place of immense natural wealth, unaware that explorers are now reaching your shores and penetrating your sanctuary—explorers who are here to take control of what you possess and to dispossess you.

This is nature. This is evolution. This is what happens when the native peoples of any place or world squander their resources and are not prepared for intervention. This is not to say that humanity will, by destiny, fall under foreign power. But it is the great risk you now face—the great, unrecognized risk, the great background to the Great Waves of change, the hidden threat to humanity.

If the nations of the world knew this, they would unite to defend the world. They would unite to protect the world's resources so that humanity will have a future. For do not think that you can go out into space and claim what you have destroyed or overused here on Earth. You would have great difficulty finding these resources, and even if you could eventually find them, you would find that they are owned by others—others who are far more powerful than you are.

There is so much foolishness, recklessness and adolescence in human behavior that must be corrected. The New Message warns of this, admonishes this and speaks of this. You cannot be foolish and arrogant in the Greater Community. And you can no longer be foolish and arrogant even within your own world.

This is a time of great reckoning when humanity will have to either grow up and unite or fail and be overtaken by others. If you do not accept this, if you cannot accept this, if this is too much for you, if you think it is untrue, then you are ignorant and weak. This is the Revelation. Ignore it at your own

If the nations of the world knew this, they would unite to defend the world.

At present, humanity is a weak and divided steward of a beautiful planet that is highly prized by others.

risk. For even God will not save you if you do not honor and pay heed to God's warnings.

Countless times have emerging races such as your own been overtaken by resource explorers and economic collectives—those who search for opportunities such as this, those who are predatory, those who are opportunistic, those who can gain control over worlds like this without firing a shot.

You are entering a much more sophisticated and powerful environment in the Greater Community where outright war is rare, but where deception and the attempt to control are immense. You do not yet have wisdom, for you have not had to adapt to this greater environment. But wisdom from the Greater Community is being provided to you in the New Message. And you have allies in the Universe who have sent their warnings, their perspective and their information to help you to prepare for the Greater Community and to warn you of the dangers of depleting your Earth and of throwing away your self-sufficiency.

The picture is actually very clear. It is not complex. If you fail to take care of this place, others from the Universe will come and displace you. They will not destroy you. They will simply harness you and use you, the way you use cattle, the way humanity has used slaves. It is not a complex situation. Even your children could understand it. It has happened throughout nature and throughout the Greater Community since time began, since the Separation from God began.

The fact that people do not see it, do not think of it, do not recognize it, cannot imagine it or cannot face it simply represents your lack of development, your lack of wisdom and the indulgences that you have given yourself to that blind you to the realities of the basic laws of nature itself.

Therefore, you must face the Great Waves of change; you

must face the Greater Community—not with preference and not with fear, but with strength and objectivity. And you must gain this strength and this objectivity, which Knowledge within you will give you, for it is not afraid. Knowledge has no preferences beyond the great truth it is here to serve.

At present, humanity is a weak and divided steward of a beautiful planet that is highly prized by others. How will you protect it? How will you defend it? How will you maintain its wealth and its diversity of life? If you squander it, you will lose it, and the costs will be beyond your imagination. If you fall under foreign persuasion, it will create a set of circumstances far worse than anything you could imagine.

This is life. You must grow up to be in life. You must prepare for eventualities. Nature is unmerciful to the unprepared. Both history and nature teach you what happens when these preparations are not made. You must be sober and clear, and then you can enjoy life, be in life and be secure in life. But you cannot gain pleasures away from this without jeopardizing your position, and at present, humanity's position is in great jeopardy.

Great decisions will have to be made as to how humanity will proceed—decisions both at the level of government and leadership and at the level of each person. Will you fight and struggle for what you want, to hold onto what you have, or will you unite with others to provide a greater stability in your communities, in your towns, your cities and your nations? Will you accept the reality of the Great Waves of change, or will you continue to deny them, projecting onto life your preferences, your dreams, your fantasies and the assurances that your indulgences can be maintained indefinitely? Will you deny the reality of the Greater Community even though the Intervention is flying in your skies and taking

You must prepare for eventualities. Nature is unmerciful to the unprepared.

This is the time for humanity to unite and to become strong. The incentive for this is immense.

your people against their will? Will you remain foolish and ignorant, like the adolescent, unwilling to face reality, unwilling to face the responsibility, unwilling to serve anyone but yourself? These are the questions. This is the challenge.

God has provided a New Message for humanity to warn humanity of the Great Waves of change, to warn humanity of intervention from the Greater Community and to teach that humanity has a greater spiritual power called Knowledge that represents its core strength, both on an individual and a collective level, and that humanity must use this Knowledge and its own native abilities to restore the world and to establish itself as a free and self-determined race in the Universe.

Though humanity has a great destiny, its future is now in great danger. Do not take it for granted that humanity will succeed. Do not think that your success is somehow guaranteed. Do not assume that no matter what happens, humanity will emerge and be able to continue. Do not think that your ascendancy in this world guarantees your future self-determination.

To assume these things is to maintain your weakness and avoid your strength. For strength always arises in facing reality, not in running away from it. And reality will either serve you or undermine you, depending upon the position you take with it.

This is the time for humanity to unite and to become strong. The incentive for this is immense. The possibility for failure is great. This is your chance to rise or to fall, to become great, united and free in the Universe or to diminish yourselves here on Earth and fall under subjugation to foreign powers. This represents the great threshold for humanity, the great opportunity for humanity and the great challenge for humanity.

CHAPTER 10

The Great Waves and the Hidden Reality of Contact

Part of the Great Waves of change for humanity is that it must face the reality that it is not alone in the Universe or even within its own world. For expeditionary forces from the Greater Community, from the physical Universe, are in the world today and have been here for some time—interfering in human affairs, manipulating human perception, promoting human conflict, acting surreptitiously behind the scenes, taking people against their will and subjecting them to often terrible experiments, turning their minds so that they will become supportive and allegiant to this Intervention.

While you have been living your life under normal circumstances, great things have been going on behind the scenes—things that the public has no idea of. And though many people have seen craft flying in their skies and countless sightings have been reported, the mystery of this presence in your world has remained undercover, behind the scenes, out of public view.

Great effort has been taken by many of your governments to discourage any inquiry into this, creating a veil of secrecy and ridicule that has been quite effective in discouraging public conversation and public awareness of this great encounter, this great challenge to human freedom. No government will admit to its people that it is facing an adversary for which it has no adequate response.

Into the world at this time when the Great Waves are beginning to emerge have come other forces—competitors from the Universe.

So the mystery of this has now been covered up by lies and deception. People have been encouraged to believe fantastic things about the alien presence in the world, thinking that it is a fantasy or that it represents some kind of wonderful story from the past. It is now so veiled in half-truths and deception, in ridicule and in fantasy, that even those people who have recognized a foreign presence in the world cannot think clearly about it. It has been so confused, so muddled, so turned and so changed. Certain people have even been encouraged by the governments to tell fantastic and wild stories, to create discredit upon anyone who might seek to present anything true or real or to attempt to generate an honest conversation, a public conversation, a public debate, a public awareness.

Into the world at this time when the Great Waves are beginning to emerge have come other forces—competitors from the Universe. They come not with weapons. They come not with an armada of vessels. They come with the power of persuasion and deception. Their technology is advanced, but what they rely upon is their ability to influence the minds of those who live here. In this Greater Community of intelligent life in the Universe, war as it is known within this world is actually far more rare than you might realize. Other ways have been found to overcome opponents: trickery, deception, manipulation, projection and power in the mental environment—an environment that humanity knows almost nothing about.

While influence is attempted in every household, in every nation, influence in the Greater Community has taken on far greater and more subtle demonstrations and is far more powerful as well. Those races who are seeking to gain access to the world want to preserve its resources. They see humanity as one of the resources. They are not here to destroy you, but to use you—to use your intelligence and your strength, to use you to serve them. And they will take whatever time is required, using extremely subtle means to achieve this end.

The world is so valuable. It is so rich biologically, and it has such a great and important strategic position. You do not realize what a prize this world is and how valued it is to those few races that are aware of it and who seek it for themselves. They will compete for it, but they will use similar means and tactics.

They will attempt to weaken the strongest nations by engaging them in intractable conflicts, by encouraging the overuse of the resources of the world—resources that they themselves do not need. They will spread discontent. They will promote the idea that human leadership cannot save the world, that humanity is essentially destructive and that only a foreign power—only the power of the Intervention—can save humanity from itself, from destroying itself, from destroying its world and from succumbing to the Great Waves of change.

You now have competitors from beyond. They are not warriors. They do not conquer through force. Their powers are subtle but extremely effective in a world where people are divided and in conflict with one another, in a world where people are ignorant of the realities and requirements of life in the Universe around them, in a world where people are superstitious, in a world where people have not yet learned to trust the deeper Knowledge that God has placed within them.

All of these things make you vulnerable to persuasion and manipulation. And while the Intervention will seek to remain hidden and out of view for the majority of the people in the world, those who are aware of its presence will be influenced. Many will be taken and their minds will be turned towards the Intervention. Many will be used for reproductive experiments.

You do not realize what a prize this world is and how valued it is to those few races that are aware of it and who seek it for themselves.

Many will be taken and never returned to this world.

It is so fantastic, it is so incredible that people can hardly believe that something like this could happen. Yet people have forgotten that they are a part of nature, that competition and intervention are parts of nature, that species try to compete with each other for environment and for resources. Humanity now has reached a position of power and has developed a worldwide infrastructure that foreign races can use. Humanity is facing the Great Waves of change. So it is uniquely vulnerable to the kind of influence and persuasion that will be presented here.

People will say, "This is incredible. I do not believe this." But you must ask yourself who has been flying in your skies for the past many decades? Who has been churning panic among your governments for the past many decades? And why would nations act so foolishly, outstripping their resources and engaging in conflicts with others, conflicts that cannot be won? You may say it is human greed and foolishness, but that is not sufficient. For humanity is at a great turning point, a turning point that will lead either to its permanent decline or to its future ascension as a united and powerful race.

It is at this great threshold that certain other races will exert their influence because the resources of the world are valuable and because humanity is viewed as a resource by these forces. Great care will be taken to encourage a shift in authority, a reliance upon foreign power, a reliance upon foreign technology. All the while, the Intervention will present itself as a benign and uplifting force to those few people who have become aware of it and especially to those who have come under its influence.

This complicates your situation. It indeed creates a great barrier of recognition for people. So much confusion, deception and ridicule have been planted now in the human awareness that people—especially in the more wealthy nations—are afraid to even think about these things, thinking that if they do so, they will be foolish; they will appear foolish to others.

That is why a New Message has to be given now, for humanity is at the critical turning point which will determine whether it will be a failing civilization, a failing race in a world that will eventually come under foreign power and domination, or whether it will exercise its greater intelligence, its greater power, to become a united and free race within a Greater Community of intelligent life in the Universe.

You must see that you are the native peoples of this world and learn the lessons of intervention. Learn the lessons that have taught you what has happened to native peoples when they encountered forces from beyond their awareness, forces displaying different and perhaps greater technology, forces that they did not understand, forces that they mistook for some kind of spiritual entity or spiritual emissary.

History tells you how great civilizations have capitulated to small groups of clever and deceptive invaders. Especially later in the history of the world, this has been demonstrated repeatedly. Entire nations and cultures, even today, are falling under persuasion of foreign powers by dependence on foreign technology and by the persuasion of the Intervention itself.

Now all of humanity is facing this. Now all of humanity represents the native peoples of this world facing intervention by small expeditionary forces who are here to begin to turn humanity against itself to gain influence, to gain ascendancy, to unite with people psychologically and emotionally and, in some cases, even biologically. In this way, humanity could be overtaken without any signs of overt violence. This is how a more intelligent and united race overtakes a much larger but weaker and divided race.

Now all of humanity represents the native peoples of this world facing intervention.

You are now facing skills you have not yet cultivated. You are now facing a deception that is doubly difficult to discern because of the Intervention's intentions to deceive and because of the difficulty and confusion that human beings themselves have sown around this most fundamental and consequential event.

The Creator of all life will not allow humanity to simply be overtaken through deception, through guile, through manipulation without a great warning. The New Message has given this warning. It has even called upon your potential allies in the Universe to send spies to view this Intervention and to give their report. These spies have never visited the Earth, but they have witnessed the Intervention and have sent their report in a series of Briefings from the Allies of Humanity. You do not know who these races are, but their testimony is essential for your development and preparation for the Greater Community.

When you put all these pieces together, the picture becomes very clear. The human family is now struggling—facing a world in decline, facing a world of diminishing resources, facing the ever greater risk of competition, conflict and war amongst its divided nations and peoples. Into this, competitors come to use these situations to their advantage and to prey upon human weakness, superstition and conflict.

If you could look at the history of humanity, particularly the recent history of humanity, where other alternatives to force have been used to gain control of other nations and peoples, you will see that the Intervention today is following a very familiar pattern. It is just that humanity is not used to being in this position. It believes it is ascendant. It believes it is powerful. It does not recognize that another race could come and take advantage of its weakness, its conflicts and its superstitions.

All of these circumstances work against you now, and that is why a New Message has been sent into the world to warn and prepare humanity for the Great Waves of change and for the reality of encountering a Greater Community of intelligent life.

People do not know anything about life in the Universe, and that is why this education is so fundamental and essential. Even your great scientists would think that anyone who would come to visit would be fascinated with humanity, would want to share science with humanity, would want to share technology with humanity and would want to help humanity. And yet, in reality, the first races that you will encounter directly will be resource explorers and economic collectives, those who are here to take advantage of an immense opportunity and who will take advantage of your place in history, your circumstances, your tendencies and your ignorance.

This warning about the Intervention must be part of your education now, or you will underestimate the power of the times in which you live. You will underestimate the power and the dangers of the Great Waves of change and how they can be used against you by others whom you do not recognize.

These visitors to the world are not multidimensional beings. They are not from the spirit world. They are not angels or demons. They are physical beings like you, driven by the same needs that drive humanity—the need for resources, the need for control, the need for wealth and the need for stability.

There is no one in the world who can give you a Greater Community education, who can provide to you wisdom from the Greater Community. This really must come from God. Part of this preparation must come from those few races who are aware of you,

> *This warning about the Intervention must be part of your education now, or you will underestimate the power of the times in which you live.*

who could be your future allies, for their testimony is crucial to your understanding. In the greater nature of things, advanced and successful races must pass on their wisdom to emerging worlds such as your own, and they must do this without actually interfering in these worlds.

This represents a greater tradition in the Universe than you are yet aware of. But you are now the beneficiaries of this, and such a gift of wisdom must be given without manipulation and without intervention. That is why those races who are intervening in the world today represent those who would seek to take advantage of a weak and divided humanity.

The emphasis now must not be on the national security for one nation alone, but on security for the entire world.

You must have great strength to face this. You must be able to gather the courage within yourself to face this. If you make a mistake here, if you do not recognize your situation and your opposition, then you will make a great and perhaps fatal error. That is why this gift from God, this gift of profound love and regard for humanity, must be given with great urgency and great seriousness.

You do not realize what a prize you are living on, this beautiful world, and how rare such worlds are in the Universe, and how advanced technological nations have outstripped their home worlds and must now search and travel for resources. In fact, this is not a mystery. This is part of nature, nature that you can understand. The history of the Universe is not so different from the history of your world, where the strong will dominate the weak if they can.

This is why you cannot be complacent. You cannot be foolish and self-indulgent. You cannot be lazy and indolent in the face of either the Great Waves of change or this Intervention from the Greater Community in which you live.

This represents the great warning that the New Message is providing. Yet the New Message provides a blessing and a preparation, for humanity has the power to offset this Intervention and to face and navigate the difficult times ahead within your world.

Humanity has sown the seeds of its own demise through misuse and overuse of the world, but this can be mitigated to a great degree, and adaptation can occur. But to do this, humanity will have to unite. It will have to end its ceaseless conflicts and prepare to face a world in decline and to face competition from the Greater Community.

Here your times have the power to either defeat you or to unite you and uplift you. The decision rests not only with governments, but with each person—their ability to face change, to respond to change, to prepare for change, to adapt to change and to unite together for mutual security. For the emphasis now must not be on the national security for one nation alone, but on security for the entire world.

Interventions such as you are facing now will continue because you are a weak and divided race living on a beautiful planet. This will draw others here to attempt, primarily through persuasion and guile, to influence humanity to unite with them, to become dependent upon them and to trust in them. These persuasions will not cease even if this Intervention is thwarted.

It is like the young girl entering the big city, thinking that everyone will be her friend, not having an idea of how she could be preyed upon and taken advantage of, and all of the myriad persuasions that can be placed upon her to acquiesce, to give herself over. This is the complexity and challenge of living in physical reality.

Yet God has given you a deeper Knowledge that cannot be manipulated, that cannot be persuaded and that cannot fall under any kind of persuasion, whether its source be human or from beyond the world. Knowledge within you only responds to

God and to Knowledge within others. It cannot be manipulated, it cannot be persuaded, and that is why it represents your greatest strength—your core strength, the most reliable aspect of yourself. That is why Knowledge and the emergence of Knowledge will play a key role in determining the outcome for humanity, which at this moment remains unsure and unresolved. Knowledge is the most powerful force in the Universe, and the Intervention is not using it, or it would not be intervening here.

Humanity has a rich spiritual heritage despite its many errors. You do not realize what a great advantage you have in these initial encounters with life in the Universe. You do not recognize your strengths. It is your weaknesses that will be preyed upon by this Intervention and by any future interventions. That is why it is your strength that must be encouraged, that must be revealed and that must be shared, acknowledged and brought to bear. That is what the New Message emphasizes.

You have no idea how to prepare for the Greater Community. There is no one in the world who knows how to do this. Either a foreign power could teach you this or God could teach you this. However, a foreign power would be unlikely to do that unless they had a special interest here, unless they had designs of their own. So the message must come from God. Those Allies who have sent their wisdom will not intervene. For the truth is humanity is not ready to encounter beneficial races in the Universe. You do not have the unity. You do not have the power. You do not have the discernment or the wisdom. And you do not yet have the discretion.

Real beneficial contact with life in the Universe may not happen until humanity has faced and overcome the Great Waves of change. But in the interim, others will attempt to intervene, to take advantage of increasing human conflict and uncertainty, the uncertainty and conflict that can be generated by the Great Waves of change themselves.

Do not fall into the trap of thinking that this is about love or fear. That is a fool's discernment. It is about wisdom or no wisdom. It is about responsibility or irresponsibility. It is about seeing the truth or not seeing the truth. It is about responding to reality or not responding to reality.

Eventually, you will have to overcome your fear to gain a greater strength and a greater objectivity. But that is the goal. To reach this position of clarity and strength, you must face the great threshold that all humanity is now encountering. You must prepare for it, and you must outgrow your childish fantasies and your foolish distractions.

Particularly in the wealthy nations, people who have been used to losing themselves in their pleasures, their hobbies and their addictions must now awaken to the reality that their preeminence in the world is being challenged and that the Earth itself will not be able to provide for them what they are used to receiving from it.

Do not think that any foreign power would come here to try to help you without wanting something from you.

The poorer people of the world understand deprivation. They understand intervention. They understand manipulation, for they have been living under it and suffering under it for so very long. It is the wealthy people who are ignorant, who are blinded. It is they who must bring to bear the strengths of humanity. It is they who must unite the nations to preserve human freedom and sovereignty in this world and to assure that human civilization does not crumble under the weight and the force of the Great Waves of change.

You must hear the power of this message. You must have strength of heart. You must have courage. If you run away, there will be no place to hide, and you will only weaken your position, making you more vulnerable in the future. Time now is of the essence—time to see, time to know, time to prepare and time to encourage human unity and human freedom. You do this not only for its own merits, but to secure humanity's ability to face the Great Waves of change and to face an Intervention that to this day operates with very little human awareness and very little human resistance.

Do not think that any foreign power would come here to try to help you without wanting something from you. Do not think any foreign power would extend itself to humanity and its difficult circumstances, expending this wealth and this energy, unless they had a great and secret motive. History teaches you that intervention is always carried out for self-interest and that the races who face intervention, should they succumb, will be devastated by it and in some cases destroyed entirely.

You have seen this in your history. It is known in your world. It is part of your experience of life and of nature. You must be realistic. You must be honest. The situation is not as confusing as you think it is. The cloud of confusion is perpetrated by forces both human and alien who seek to keep humanity out of the picture, who want to keep humanity divided, weak and unresponsive. But the picture itself can be easily seen if you have the courage to see and the right information and understanding.

But it creates a deceptive environment, this Intervention. It has many human allies now who are part of its deception, who will speak of the great alien presence, its gifts of technology and its promise for humanity's future. Be very careful now. Be very careful and use discernment. Do not fall under such persuasions perpetrated by powers that have never revealed their true purpose and meaning, that function here in secret, that are engaged in many activities, many of which are nefarious in nature. Reserve your judgment until you can learn and see more clearly.

The blessing that the New Message is presenting is the recognition and assurance that humanity has a greater power, the power of Knowledge. Humanity has a long tradition of religion and spirituality that, despite its many errors, has kept humanity's ability to follow Knowledge alive and has kept compassion and giving alive in this world, whereas these things have failed in so many other worlds.

Humanity has great promise to become a free and advancing race in the Universe.

Humanity has great strengths and great promise. Religion and spirituality are still alive here in contrast to where they have died out in highly technological societies. In this, you have a gift to give to the Universe. But first you must survive the Great Waves of change. And you must survive these initial attempts at intervention into the world.

You must unite. You must be self-sufficient. And you must be extremely discreet. These are the three requirements for any world or association of worlds to establish if they are to be free and self-determined in a Universe full of greater persuasions, in a Universe where competition is taking place on a scale you cannot even imagine.

It is time for humanity to grow up, to unite and to become strong. It is time for humanity to cease to be a weak and divided steward of a beautiful planet and to become strong and united for the preservation of the world and for the preservation and advancement of human freedom and sovereignty here.

God has given you this world to provide everything you need. Should you exhaust your natural inheritance, you will have to seek what you need from other powers in the Universe. If this occurs, you will lose much of your freedom and self-determination, becoming only a client state to foreign powers, who will not hesitate to take advantage of your weakened, dependent position.

This gift is a gift of love. It is a gift that comes with great urgency. It calls to a greater Knowledge and sobriety within you. Your intellect—your thinking, personal mind that has been so conditioned by the world—may argue against it, may contend against it, may refuse it, may deny it, may try to compare it with other things or may try to unite it with other things. But this communication is for a deeper part of you, the part of you that cannot be fooled and that is not foolish, the part of you that is strong, the part of you that is naturally compassionate, the part of you that is united and capable of union with others.

Humanity has great promise to become a free and advancing race in the Universe. But to achieve this, it must face the results of its own misuse of the world. It must unite. It must become strong, and it must care for this world so that its self-sufficiency can be maintained into the future.

Only if you can achieve this will beneficial contact with other races be possible. And even here you will need to exercise great discernment and discretion. For freedom in the Universe is rare. Free and self-determined races in the Universe are rare. In this, you do not realize the great advantages that you already possess in the limited freedom that you have been able to establish here in this world and how much it has produced a benefit for humankind.

This is the world you have come to serve. It may not be what you want it to be, but it is right for why you are really here, for you have come with a greater purpose and a mission. You have come to make specific contributions to the world in concert with certain other people. This represents your greater purpose, not the purpose that your imagination creates or that your society emphasizes, but the greater purpose that is born of your union with God.

You have come into the world facing Great Waves of change and Intervention. This is the world you have come to serve. If you cannot recognize it, if you cannot face it, then your service will never be valued and never be rendered. Therefore, the first great threshold is to face the great threshold. And that is why this Message, this preparation for the Greater Community and for the Great Waves of change are being given to you now.

CHAPTER 11

Where Will You Place Your Faith?

FAITH IS IMPORTANT IF IT IS BUILT upon experience. Without experience as its foundation, faith becomes merely a hope, and hope alone is weak. It does not have the power to face disappointment and uncertainty sufficiently.

To have faith in God will depend upon one's expectations. What do you expect from God? What do you want from God? What are you willing to give to God?

Though faith itself can cover a broad range of experience, its value can be determined, then, upon what the motives are behind it, what the expectations are and what one expects or even demands of God.

People are very disappointed in God because certain expectations are not met. These individuals have experienced loss, the loss of loved ones or disappointment and failure. They have experienced tragedy, and now their notion and their confidence that God exists is shaken and sometimes even destroyed.

People will have faith in something because to have faith is natural. If they do not have faith in God, they will have faith in something else that takes the place of God. They may have faith in their government. They may have faith in the economy. They may have faith in industry. They may have faith in themselves and their abilities. They may have faith in certain individuals. They may have faith in nature. But whatever it is, they will have faith. To be without faith is to be without relationship, and to be without relationship is to live in hell.

The question then becomes what does one have faith in and what is the nature of that faith? Is it built upon real experience, or is it built upon ideas or philosophy? Is this faith well placed, and does it have real strength to it?

In face of the Great Waves of change that are coming to the world, which will challenge people's faith in themselves, in their nation, in nature itself and in God, the question of faith becomes very important. The strength of this faith and where it is placed become very significant in terms of the individual's ability not only to function, but to be creative, discerning and competent in the face of changing circumstances.

If you have faith in government, you will see the government's inability to provide. The government will appear to be conflicted and in some cases incompetent—unable to meet the situation, unable to educate the people and unable to guide the people. Indeed, this is already the case. Who amongst the governments is telling the truth about the Great Waves of change—about the real situation regarding energy resources, the real potential of a changing and heating climate, the danger of pandemic illness, the growing competition that is occurring over who will gain access to the remaining resources, the real potential for economic instability and the condition of the economic situation?

People will have faith in their religion, but their religion is not educating them, preparing them or guiding their attention correctly.

Other people will have faith in nature, but nature will prove to be harsh, exacting and even unmerciful to the unprepared.

Others will have faith in God, but they will be challenged with the question of how could God allow such great change to occur? Where is Providence? Where is God's guiding hand? Where is the blessing?

As times become more difficult, people will be thrown into very difficult circumstances. There will be tragedy. There will be starvation. There will be conflict. How could a loving God allow this to happen? Is God punishing humanity for its errors? Or is God simply allowing humanity to reap the reward of its errors? What kind of loving Creator would do that, particularly in the face of tragedy and deprivation?

People's faith in themselves will be greatly challenged as they are faced with circumstances they did not anticipate and for which they are not prepared. This will be particularly difficult for the wealthy, who now have to face very difficult decisions and the prospect of losing much of their wealth.

What will happen to people's faith in life itself? Now life is taking a radical turn. It seems to be going into a chaotic state. Change and difficulty are happening in an ever-accelerating manner. How can one have faith in life when it is becoming so unpredictable and in many places so very hazardous?

People's faith in themselves will be greatly challenged as they are faced with circumstances they did not antici-pate and for which they are not prepared.

People's faith will be greatly challenged. That is why it is necessary and has always been necessary to place your faith in the guiding power that God has placed within you—the power and the presence of Knowledge—the deeper intelligence that is here to guide you, to protect you and to lead you, if you are willing to follow, to a greater life and a greater contribution to others.

Knowledge remains so undiscovered and so unexpressed, except by only a few and rare individuals, that people really do not know what it is capable of. They think that Knowledge is their mind that they think with, but who can have faith in one's intelligence when one is faced with such confounding and seemingly irresolvable problems?

The intellect will not have answers now. It will blame. It will complain. It will go into denial. It may become terrified if

What will you have faith in within such a radically changing world? In your government? In your financial institutions? In the marketplace? In your religious institutions?

it actually has to face reality. But it within itself is not capable of dealing with the power and the consequences of the Great Waves of change. Knowledge remains unknown and unrecognized. People can recognize some of its manifestations and call it intuition. But it is greater than this.

What will you have faith in within such a radically changing world? In your government? In your financial institutions? In the marketplace? In your religious institutions? Will you have faith in nature? Will you have faith in the intellect? Will you have faith in certain individuals, who may well appear to be completely confounded by the changing circumstances that you all share? Will you have faith in change? Everything is changing. Life is changing. Will you have faith in enlightenment, that you will become enlightened beyond the specter of love and fear, hope and despair—an enlightenment that is so difficult to achieve and so rarely achieved? Will you have faith in your spiritual path, which for most people will not prepare them for the Great Waves of change? What will you have faith in? Have you lost faith already, becoming ever more helpless and hopeless, even before the Great Waves have really begun to strike?

Some people have faith in hopelessness. That is what they believe in. That is what they think is inevitable. Some people have faith in romance, and so they live in a kind of romantic dreamland, as if their life were a movie of some kind, disassociated from everything around them and from everything real within themselves.

The real challenge here is to have faith in Knowledge, to take the steps to Knowledge and to learn what Knowledge is—

to experience it, to recall the experiences you have already had of it, to see that it is the constant thread of your life through times that were happy and times that were difficult, through changing circumstances and through changing relationships. Through moments of success and moments of despair, there is this thread of Knowledge—this constant thread, this constant presence, this constant and abiding intelligence that is beneath and beyond your intellect.

God has placed this perfect guiding intelligence within you. Ultimately, what else can you have faith in except faith in Knowledge within yourself and within other people? Knowledge is not confined by changing circumstances. It does not have the fallibility of the intellect. It is not threatened by death and destruction. It is not attached to pleasures and people, places and things. It is unconcerned with wealth and the loss of wealth. It is here on a mission, a mission from God. Its mission is your mission, waiting to be discovered.

Everything around you will be challenged. Everything around you will prove to be weak, fallible and vulnerable. Institutions will be overwhelmed and in some cases will fail. Nature will appear to be harsh and uncompromising. The hope for Providence or for being rescued will fade as times continue. This will be a crisis of faith for so many people. Yet in reality you were sent into the world to live in this time, to face these circumstances and to contribute something unique and essential that only Knowledge within you knows.

The Great Waves of change are a tragedy for the intellect. They are a tragedy for your personal mind and idea of yourself. But for Knowledge, they are the ideal circumstance. They are the challenge Knowledge has been

You were sent into the world to live in this time, to face these circumstances and to contribute something unique and essential.

waiting for. They are the greatest opportunity for contribution and the opportunity to create a new foundation for humanity and a new way forward for humanity. Knowledge is the core of your strength. It is the most powerful aspect of you. It is the part of you that is connected to God. It is through Knowledge that God speaks to you.

Many people seem to think that God is here to provide a beneficial life, a set of pleasant and peaceful circumstances, as if God is managing their environment. Of course, when things go out of hand or out of control, tragedy strikes or the social structure breaks down, then faith in God is thrown into immense doubt and confusion.

Even if you have to make a thousand turns in your life, Knowledge will guide you to make the right turns.

Some people think that God guarantees happiness and satisfaction. When happiness and satisfaction do not exist, people are either being unfaithful or somehow God is failing them and their unquestioned and often unconscious expectations.

God knows the world is a difficult and hazardous place. That is why God has placed Knowledge within you. It is this mysterious intelligence, this fleeting experience of certainty and direction, that you must place your faith in. Everything else may seem to fail or prove to be fallible or inadequate, but Knowledge lives within you. It is mysterious because you cannot define it, you cannot control it and you cannot use it. It is not a tool of the intellect. You cannot use it to become wealthy, to dominate others or to destroy your enemies.

It is far more powerful than the intellect. It is free of the intellect. It is only hampered by the intellect in the sense that your mind and your thoughts create in most cases obstacles to your experiencing the power and the presence of Knowledge.

Only Knowledge will know what to do in the face of ever-increasing uncertainty. Even if you have to make a thousand turns in your life, Knowledge will guide you to make the right turns. What else can do this for you? Who else has this wisdom and this equanimity to guide you in this manner?

Many people will be looking to their government leaders to provide safety and security, and great attempts will be made to provide this safety and security. But you cannot live upon this hope alone. For the government will have limited resources, and the strain upon government institutions will be so immense, they will not be able to provide for everyone.

You may need these services, but still what is guiding you is Knowledge—if you can follow it, if you yield to it, if you can open your mind to allow this presence to be there and to learn to build a connection to Knowledge. Not only will it save you from catastrophe, from dangerous situations, from making self-destructive decisions and from following people who will lead you into greater difficulty, but it will give you the strength and confidence you need.

You cannot have faith that everything will turn out all right, for many people will fail.

Ultimately, the very circumstances that seem so threatening, overwhelming or disconcerting are the very circumstances that will enable your true gifts to come forward. That is because Knowledge has come into the world to meet these circumstances. To you, it was unexpected. To your idea of yourself and your intellect, it was unexpected. It is perceived as catastrophic or tragic, a great misfortune. But for Knowledge, it is the perfect set of circumstances where you outgrow selfishness, weakness, self-abuse and personal addiction in order to rise to a great occasion.

You cannot have faith in the occasion because the occasion itself is very changeable. It is not certain exactly how things will occur, how people will respond and what will happen.

Many false leaders will arise in times of great difficulty and much bad information and guidance will be offered.

Circumstances may conspire against you. You cannot have faith in them. You cannot have faith that everything will turn out all right, for many people will fail, and tragic consequences are very possible. You cannot have faith that you will make it through because you do not know that you will make it through. Without Knowledge, you will not have this confidence or this certainty.

The question of faith is very important because it will determine what you will look for within yourself and in other people. Many people will arise claiming to have the answer to lead humanity forward. They will aspire to leadership in government or religion. Yet you will be able to see whether they are guided by Knowledge or just by personal ambition. Many false leaders will arise in times of great difficulty and much bad information and guidance will be offered. Some of these individuals will truly be dangerous. Only Knowledge can tell you this.

You who are so conditioned to follow the opinions of others or to look to your immediate environment for certainty will be thrown into such confusion and even despair. Yet Knowledge within you is not confused. Knowledge is not despairing. With Knowledge, you can face any kind of changing circumstances without despair, without condemnation, without falling apart within yourself, without breaking down and without losing heart. That is why Knowledge is the most important thing in life. For you, perhaps it is a mystery, something rarely experienced, something beyond comprehension, something faint, something weak or something distant. But Knowledge is the most important thing in life.

The times ahead will destroy your faith in so many things. They will reveal your dependence upon these things and all the assumptions that are associated with them. All the things that you thought would take care of you, provide for you and assure your future will now be thrown into grave question and doubt, leading you to become cynical and despairing, hostile and angry.

Your life will be threading its way through a dense forest where there are no trails. What will guide you here? What will lead you on? If faith in everything else fails you, what will lead you on? You may have faith in your family, but your family may fall into disarray, conflict and confusion. You may have faith in your primary relationships, but these people may capitulate to fear, anger or confusion.

To have faith in others who are strong with Knowledge is valuable. But it is Knowledge within you that will give you the strength to follow them. Since no one is beyond error, the strength within you will help them to avoid error, and they will help you to avoid error. This is the power of a relationship guided by Knowledge. But it is still Knowledge at the core of each individual that makes the real difference.

To become strong with Knowledge is to shift your allegiance to Knowledge and to build a foundation of experience in Knowledge so that now your faith in Knowledge is not simply a hope, a wish or a presumption. It is now based upon a growing body of experience. This is faith justified.

However, faith itself should never be blind. You cannot become passive and think that Knowledge will guide you through everything, and you simply just have to follow along like a little child. You will have to bring your intellect to bear and all of your senses, all of your skills and all of your attention. You will have to

Your life will be threading its way through a dense forest where there are no trails. What will guide you here? What will lead you on?

People have placed their faith inappropriately in so many things that they cannot imagine change on a great scale.

go through life and face these challenges as if you were walking on a very icy street—walking carefully, looking carefully, bringing all of your faculties to bear.

You cannot drift into a kind of welfare mentality and think that God will just give you everything you need without any effort on your part, for this will certainly not be the case. Every aspect of yourself, all of your strengths and your faculties will have to be brought to bear. This is in part what redeems you so that you are made whole. You are made complete. Instead of being a mass of different sub-personalities, different ambitions or conflicting goals, you are now brought into one focus, guided by one mind, organized and focused to meet challenging circumstances. Here challenging circumstances are redemptive to you and ultimately to nations of people.

You will have to make very big decisions in the face of the Great Waves of change, perhaps bigger than anything you have ever done. You will have to guide others who are far weaker than you, who do not have this strength or this faith in Knowledge. How will you do it? You cannot vacillate endlessly. You cannot be ambivalent. You cannot be indecisive for very long. You will have to make really big decisions, act upon them and overcome your self-doubt, your fear and your anxiety. What will give you the strength to do this? Faith in human leadership? Faith in human institutions? Faith in a distant God?

People have placed their faith inappropriately in so many things that they cannot imagine change on a great scale. People have faith in technology, thinking that technology will solve all the problems that technology creates and that people create. It will be a new gadget or a new source of energy, and everything will be fine. You will just transition into the next energy paradigm, with a little discomfort and a little uncertainty along the way. People think that technology is now their god. Technology will provide for them and save them, giving them stability, wealth and power.

Technology will be overwhelmed by the Great Waves of change. New technology will have to be developed, but it alone cannot save people. The power of nature will always overwhelm technology. This is a lesson that has been forgotten by people living in modern times. The marvels of technology have given you many conveniences and have provided medicines that have saved people's lives. But in the face of the Great Waves of change, this technology may not be available. It may not be produced to meet new needs. It will not be available to everyone. And in certain cases it will be inadequate.

Without sufficient petroleum, how will you run your cars, your farm machinery, your transportation system and your government? Many people have faith that there is unlimited petroleum in the world. It is a faith. It is a hope. It is a wish. It is an expectation. But they have no certainty. They have never studied the problem. They do not realize that humanity will be facing declining resources. They have faith that all of these resources are there. You just spend more money, and the resources are there. You spend more money, you get more resources—endless resources. It is never a problem really.

That is a foolish faith. If one looks at the history of humanity's existence, it is a foolish faith. It is a fantasy. Yet many people live in this fantasy, base their lives on this fantasy, never question this fantasy and have absolute faith in this fantasy. Government leaders and leaders of commerce have absolute faith in this fantasy.

Many people will think the Great Waves of change are acts of God, and what will happen to their faith in God as a result? The Great Waves of change are the product of human behavior and

Technology will be overwhelmed by the Great Waves of change.

humanity's impact upon the world. Do you think this would have no consequence? Do you think the Earth can endlessly absorb such overuse and abuse without being greatly affected, without changing into a different kind of stability, without radical change?

Some people have faith that the Earth will not change and that humanity cannot change the world or disrupt the world. Many people have faith in this, and yet the world is changing and is being disrupted. And it is only the beginning.

This will free you from the paralyzing grip of fear and will enable you to take great and dramatic action while others are frozen, unable to respond.

Wherever you look, people have faith in things they do not understand. They have expectations which can never be fulfilled. It is a hope, a dream, an aspiration that goes unquestioned. Faith appears to be extremely unintelligent in light of all this—foolish, based on fantasy and expectation. Yet everyone must have faith in something because everyone must serve something. Humanity has faith, naturally. It is where this faith is placed, and the expectations that it contains, that is the critical question.

You must have faith in Knowledge primarily—Knowledge within yourself and Knowledge within others—because that is what is truly powerful. Everything else may be thrown into question, confusion and doubt. But you must come back to what is essential and what is eternal, to what comes from God directly.

This is the Great Faith. This is the power and the presence of Knowledge. This is the great thread of truth in your life. Build your strength here, and the future will not seem so overwhelming. It will not seem so threatening. You can face uncertainty with greater strength and determination. You have the power to change your circumstances in advance of great change and in the face of great change.

This represents a shift in your allegiance. It is the necessary change within yourself. This will give you equanimity, strength and courage because Knowledge is not afraid. This will free you from being bound by the opinions and the behavior of others. It will free you from the immense discouragement and disappointment that you will feel and that will exist all around you as people's faith in all other things begins to fail. This will free you from the paralyzing grip of fear and will enable you to take great and dramatic action while others are frozen, unable to respond.

This is the Great Faith. This is why that which is ineffable and mysterious represents your greatest hope and promise. All human effort guided by Knowledge, all human invention guided by Knowledge and all human ingenuity guided by Knowledge has power, direction and real promise.

Your question, then, is where will you place your faith? Where is your faith placed even right now? What will give you true strength, confidence, courage and determination? What will give you the power to overcome your own weaknesses, your own ambition, your own inhibition and your fear of disapproval by others? What will give you the power to overcome your social conditioning to meet a greater need and a greater set of problems? What will keep you above fear and hopelessness?

There is a deeper power within you. It is necessary to find this power now while you have time to build a connection to it and to allow its strength and its purpose to be revealed to you as you prepare for the Great Waves of change. This power will guide your deep evaluation and enable you to gain the vision to look out over the horizon of your life to see what is coming— to think ahead, to look ahead and to plan ahead.

To have faith in God is to have faith in the Knowledge that God has placed within you and within all other people. This is how God speaks to people. This is how God moves people. This is how God inspires people. This is how God contributes to a struggling humanity and to a world in need.

CHAPTER 12

Your Purpose and Destiny in a Changing World

In preparing for the Great Waves and in preparing for the Greater Community, you are preparing for your true purpose and greater mission in life. These are not merely inconveniences. These are the opportunities that you have been waiting for. For under normal circumstances, you will never find your greater purpose and mission in life. Something extraordinary must happen to call them forth from you, to create a situation where they will be needed and called for.

You cannot initiate yourself here. There must be greater forces at work, both on the physical plane and in the spiritual reality as well. So it is no accident that you have been confronted with the reality of the Great Waves of change, while others remain indifferent or ignorant regarding this. It is no accident that you have come to find this small part of the New Message for humanity, for it was arranged to be this way. You have come here as an act of destiny. This is a time of destiny.

People may look upon the Great Waves with horror or with denial, with all kinds of human reactions. They cannot see that what they are really facing is the one thing that will redeem them and give them a greater life, a greater purpose and a greater contribution.

It can take a long time to wait for the great events to call forth this greater purpose from you, and in the interim you will be attracted to establish your own purposes, to give yourself your own greater purpose, to give yourself to things that please you or excite you or inspire you. In the interim, you may become married. You may have a family. You may fill your life with people, responsibilities, obligations and so forth. But when the great opportunity comes, it is still your time of calling. If your life is encumbered, if you are being held back by people, responsibilities and obligations, then it is more difficult to respond. But the timing and the response are still fundamental.

It is no accident that you are now called to learn about life in the Greater Community, to be amongst the few who can receive this Revelation. You did not simply stumble upon it by accident. There is a purpose behind this, you see. This represents the great mystery of your life—that while you live your life at the surface, there are deeper forces at work beneath that surface.

At the surface, life looks chaotic and unpredictable. It looks mundane. There is nothing really extraordinary about it. It is full of stimulation, some of which gives pleasure and much of which gives pain. But deeper down, there are deeper currents moving your life, moving you into proximity to learn something, to see something, to respond to something—both within yourself and within the world at large. It is like the ocean, which is turbulent at the surface—swept by the winds of the world, moved by trivial forces. But at its depths, the ocean is being governed by greater forces, by planetary forces, by immense and mysterious forces that are moving water from one part of the Earth to another.

Your life is like that. At the surface, it is calm, it is turbulent, it changes from day to day, but it gives no real indication of its real movement and real purpose. From the surface of the ocean, how can you determine what the great movement of the waters really is? You cannot. You would need to have a greater wisdom, a greater insight of Knowledge here to really comprehend the fact that the water of the Earth is moving in a conveyor-like manner from one part of the globe to another—something you could not see or understand from the surface.

Your life has greater forces within you—forces that are stimulated by powers within the world and beyond the world,

At a deeper level, you were sent here on a mission, and nothing will satisfy that mission except the mission itself.

within the physical reality and beyond the physical reality. You have a purpose here, and it is related to the time in which you live and the events to come.

If everyone left it up to themselves to design a higher purpose, you would have a world full of musicians, poets, gardeners, therapists and so forth. It would be extremely passive. It would not be vital at all. It would not have any meaning.

So your greater purpose is really beyond these things. It is only the rare and exceptional person who is destined to become a great artist or musician, or a great athlete or an expert in a particular field. And these things are revealed to them as they go along. But for most people, the mystery remains, and from the surface of their lives, they cannot discern it—its meaning, its purpose or its direction.

You view yourself as a weak person, trying to survive, trying to be happy, trying to have good things and avoid bad things, trying to have relief, trying to have pleasures, trying to have opportunities. But at a deeper level, you were sent here on a mission, and nothing will satisfy that mission except the mission itself. And what will stimulate that mission within you are great events in the world and the needs of others that call it forth from you. They generate the initiation.

The need will grow in the world. The human family will come under greater duress. The calling will sound forth for many people to awaken from their sleep and their dreams of self-fulfillment—called into action and with it a deeper memory and sense of responsibility to the world.

From the surface, you cannot see this. It sounds fantastic. Perhaps it sounds good to you. Perhaps it does not. But you cannot see it from the surface, for it represents the mystery, the mystery of your life. Everything you do to try to be happy and to satisfy yourself, everything that you do that costs you so much in terms of time and energy and life force, cannot satisfy this deeper need—the need of the soul to discover your greater calling in life, to respond to it, to prepare for it, to be initiated into it and to serve it in the changing circumstances of your life.

Precisely when and how things will take place remain part of the mystery, for there are so many things that can change the opportunities or the timing of things. That is why making predictions is counterproductive. The future is always changing and shifting, and the outcome can take many appearances. But the direction is clear.

Therefore, you are not learning about the Great Waves of change just to try to run away somewhere and be safe. You are not having this being revealed to you simply so that you can fortify yourself. It really represents a greater calling. The different levels and kinds of service are countless. You do not yet know. You can only go towards something that calls to you, that is genuine. You must leave the definitions open. Do not come to conclusions. Do not proclaim a role or a title for yourself. That is always premature and is foolish.

The Great Waves will show you where you must go, how you must be, whom you must meet and how you must learn to respond to life. They will show you how to mature and how to become one person with one reference point within yourself, with one great focus and orientation, instead of a diffracted personality with many voices, with many directions, with all kinds of conflicts and opposition within yourself. You will never know your deeper nature by studying your personality or your personal history. It must be revealed to you through a greater experience and a greater involvement in the world.

Therefore, the correct and best approach is to put yourself in the position of being a learner, being a student—not making assumptions, not making proclamations, not living in definitions, but leaving the way open, leaving your life unexplained, allowing the mystery to call you and guide you forth.

For amidst all of the changing circumstances of your life now and the great changes that are to come to the world, there is still the mystery, and the mystery is what will give you clarity and direction. This is the realm where Knowledge exists. This is the realm where your Spiritual Family can communicate to you. This is where you can receive guidance. This is where you can do things that other people would never do, see things that people would never see and hear things that people would never hear—things that are important for your life and for the well-being of others.

The Great Waves will show you where you must go, how you must be, whom you must meet and how you must learn to respond to life.

Therefore, as you proceed, you must take time for stillness and inner listening. Stillness is learning how to still the mind and to focus the mind so that you can see beyond your thoughts and hear beyond your thoughts—hear what is there, see what is there and develop the ability to become objective and look with clarity, without preference or fear.

For most people, this skill is beyond their reach. But you must cultivate it. You cultivate it by carrying out important tasks, and you cultivate it by building a connection to Knowledge within yourself.

In taking the steps to Knowledge, you learn how to still the mind, how to listen within yourself and how to discern the voice and the movement of Knowledge from all the other voices in your mind—the voice of your parents, the voice of your teachers, the voice of your culture, the voice of your friends, the voice of your fear, the voice of your desire, the voice of your self-doubt, the voice of your self-criticism—all these other voices that reside within you. And then there is Knowledge.

You will have to leave part of your life open and mysterious.

The only way you can have confidence that what you are hearing and feeling is true is by building this connection and learning to discern the presence of Knowledge and the movement of Knowledge from all the other compulsions, all the other fantasies and ideas in your mind. *Steps to Knowledge* will teach you how to do this, and it will give you a great advantage.

Because you are entering very uncertain times, it is important that you learn to live without self-definitions, without trying to control events and without trying to live in conclusions. Here it will be necessary to live with the questions—the problems for which you do not have a solution and situations where you will have to work with a problem to learn how to resolve it, to learn how to meet its needs and so forth.

You will have to leave part of your life open and mysterious. The people who cannot do this will not fare well in the face of the Great Waves of change. They will not see, they will not know and they will not prepare. When change comes upon them, they will panic and be enraged and terrified.

If you are going to enter uncertain times, you must have this opening within yourself, this ability to listen, not for answers or explanations, but to listen to cultivate the ability to be inner-directed so when the moment comes when Knowledge must speak to you, you will be able to respond, and you will be able to feel the movement of that message moving you.

You practice stillness not to get anything, but to learn to be still. You learn to be still so that you can feel and listen. You listen to develop the ability to listen so that when you are out in life, Knowledge within you can speak to you, guide you and hold you back when that is necessary.

You will be dealing with very difficult circumstances and seeing great tribulation in the world as time goes on. How will you maintain your bearings? How will you keep yourself from entering into fear and panic, dread and apprehension? How will you prevent yourself from falling prey to the admonitions and the condemnations of others, which will arise all around you? How will you keep yourself from losing heart, from giving up, from feeling hopeless and defeated? When the rain is falling and the thunder is clashing, how will you be able to maintain clarity of mind and purpose?

These are all important questions for you now. They require a deeper connection to Knowledge and an openness about your life and about the future. You do not know what is going to happen. You do not know how it is going to turn out. You do not know necessarily who will do well and who will not. You cannot predict it, for you are entering times of great change and uncertainty. How will you know? You will have to be open and listen.

That is why the "Recommendations for Living in a Great Waves World" are really only beginning guidelines because everyone's circumstances will be somewhat different, and everyone has a unique mission and purpose in life to discover and to fulfill. So beyond establishing initial steps and building a basic foundation, you will have to rely upon Knowledge within yourself and Knowledge within others to navigate the changing and uncertain times ahead.

How will you keep yourself from losing heart, from giving up, from feeling hopeless and defeated?

You must learn to look without preference and without fear, with a clear mind.

What you are being given here is essential for your success. This is planting seeds of Knowledge and wisdom in you, but you must prepare. You must learn The Way of Knowledge. You must study the Great Waves. You must reevaluate your life—your relationships, your activities, your obligations and everything—and carry out the deep evaluation. You will have to be strong when others are weak. You will have to have faith when others have no faith. You will have to be compassionate in the face of tragedy.

You cannot lose yourself now. Before, being true to yourself was an advantage, but not a necessity. Here it will be both. You must learn to look without preference and without fear, with a clear mind and have this inner strength, this faith in Knowledge, this connection to God, this connection to the mystery—without making false assumptions, without believing that everything will turn out, without thinking you will be protected in all instances, for this is not the case.

That is why your inner preparation here is more significant than anything you do on the outside, for whatever you do on the outside is a temporary expedient. You cannot store food for the rest of your life. You cannot protect yourself from every event and eventuality. You cannot stockpile for decades. And there will be no place on Earth that will be entirely safe or beyond the reach of the Great Waves of change.

So you will have to become clear and resourceful, wise and inner-directed, for there will be very few on the outside who will be able to give you wise counsel. You will have to take care of your family and perhaps other people as well. You will have to take care of your health—your mental health and your physical health—and at times you will have to do things that are very courageous.

The more you value your strength and identify with it, the

more you will build confidence in the face of uncertainty. Even in the face of disaster, you will have an inner confidence, and it will not be a false confidence. It will not be something you simply tell yourself to placate yourself or to make yourself feel better. It is the power of Knowledge. That is your core strength, but it is mysterious. You cannot control it. You cannot make it give you what you want. You cannot use it as a resource. For you must serve it. Your mind is meant to serve Spirit, as your body is meant to serve your mind. You cannot use Spirit as a resource.

Your confidence must be established at a deeper level. The sense of authority in your life must be established beyond your personality and your ideas, for so many of your ideas will be challenged and will prove to be inadequate to face the future and to navigate the difficult times ahead.

That is why you must become a student of Knowledge, as well as a student of the world. You will need to suspend many of your ideas and beliefs about people and about the world. Many of your assumptions that you find to be self-comforting now will only weaken you and make it more difficult for you to see what you need to know and to do.

You do not know how it is going to turn out. But how it is going to turn out really does not matter because you are here to serve the world, and you serve the world without requiring a result. If your service is pure, if it comes from love and compassion, you give because you must give, not because you are assured of an outcome. You do it anyway. You try to bring about a good result, but in the end, you cannot control it. Then if your service to others seems to fail, you will not feel devastated. You did what you could. Like the

The more you value your strength and identify with it, the more you will build confidence in the face of uncertainty.

The sense of authority in your life must be established beyond your personality and your ideas.

physician in the field of battle taking care of the wounded soldiers, you do what you can with what you have.

You are here to serve, not to control. You are here to give, not to manipulate things to your own advantage. This gives you a kind of immunity from the effects of tragedy, which in some cases may be extremely disheartening. Other people around you will fail. They will fail to prepare. They will fail to see and know. They will fail to maintain their stability. Some will even lose their lives. You cannot fail. This is the confidence you must have, and it must be built upon Knowledge and not upon some false sense of yourself.

Those who will be able to navigate the highly uncertain times ahead must have this strength and inner guidance. If they are to benefit from these circumstances, if they are to be uplifted and strengthened by these challenges, that must be their focus.

From a personal point of view, it seems to be too much. The requirements are too great. The problems are too immense. The outcome is too tragic. From a personal perspective, you might as well just give up and go hide somewhere and hope that it all passes over, like a bad dream. You can wake up, and life can go on as you have known it. From a personal perspective, the Great Waves seem too radical, too extreme, impossible, improbable, illogical or unreasonable.

A New Message from God seems impossible and unreasonable. Even if you thought it was possible, you would think it would be something else, something lovely and beautiful, something sweet and assuring—nothing that requires you to deal with difficulties or to serve people under difficult circumstances. It should be something that would make you feel wonderful and carry you away in a blissful state.

But here is the difference between fantasy and reality. This *is* a New Message from God. This is what it looks like before it is adulterated, corrupted and wed with other things by people and turned into a political tool or used by religious institutions to establish their power and their dominance.

This is what a New Message looks like in its pure form. It is clear. It is powerful. It requires great things of people. And it gives great things to people. It has not been watered down to be acceptable to the masses. It has not been socialized so that it is socially acceptable. This is the real thing. You must be genuine in order to see it and to respond to it and to receive the power and the grace that it brings into your life.

People will consider the Messenger and think he must be powerful and produce miracles. He must be able to be flawless—without sin, without stain, without error, loving and compassionate to everyone all the time. Yet the real Messenger is a human being—fallible, prone to error—and yet strong, committed and dedicated.

If your service is pure, if it comes from love and compassion, you give because you must give, not because you are assured of an outcome.

Can you see the difference between fantasy and reality? If your life has been about building and sustaining fantasies, then the reality will escape you. You will still think in fantastic terms, and your expectations will reflect this.

You are hearing for the first time a New Message from God being presented into the world. You are reading it. It has never happened before. If you cannot receive it, if you do not believe it, if you think it is something else, then the reflection is upon you. To receive something pure, you must gain purity within yourself. It will not fit your expectations or the expectations of your culture and society.

The real emissaries are never valued in their lifetime. Only after they have died and are no longer a social problem or a security problem, then they are deified. Then they are exalted. Then temples and monuments are built for them. But while they were alive, they were a problem, an irritant, upsetting, disconcerting, talking about things that people had difficulty understanding or facing within themselves, setting a higher standard for life and making everyone feel how pathetically compromised their situation really is.

God has a higher regard for you than you have for yourself. Therefore, great things are given to you to do, to see and to know. If you are able to receive this and do this, you will escape your pathetic view of yourself and build a new foundation for relationship with yourself and with others as well.

The New Message brings with it a warning, a blessing and a preparation. If you do not recognize the warning, you will not understand the blessing. If you understand the warning and the blessing, you will see the need for the preparation. You will need a way, a method, a pathway to achieve and to gain the very things that are being presented here.

In the face of this, you will feel weak and confused. One day you will feel strong. The next day you will feel weak. One day you will feel that your life is blessed. The next day you will feel as if you have been deserted because that is the surface of your mind—one day calm, next day turbulent, sometimes viciously whipped up by the winds of the world, never stable. But as you learn to become connected to the power and the movement of Knowledge within yourself, this turbulence at the surface will have less and less influence over you and over your thinking and emotions. You will just see it as turbulence at the surface of your mind, and this will give you greater equanimity and objectivity.

It is not expected that you will understand the warning completely because you must keep looking yourself. You must have the comprehension yourself. To simply hear it and believe it will not be enough to stimulate courageous action within you or to evoke wisdom within you.

The blessing is that Knowledge is within you. It is here to guide you, to protect you and to lead you to your greater accomplishments in life. It is here to enable you to find the individuals who will represent a higher purpose in your life. It means that God is with you, in you, connected to you, and that humanity has a greater promise within the world and within the Greater Community of worlds. That is the blessing. And you are destined to have relationships of higher purpose if you can respond to a greater calling in your life, if you can face the reality of your life, and if you can proceed forward step by step. That is the blessing.

Those who will be able to navigate the highly uncertain times ahead must have this strength and inner guidance.

Yet it requires a very different way of considering yourself, other people, the world, the future and the past. It requires a tremendous reevaluation, and this takes time. So you will not understand the warning completely. You will not understand the blessing completely. And you will not see the need for the preparation or understand how the preparation really works.

You could look at the study of *Steps to Knowledge* and think, "Oh, this is so easy! This is basic. This is for beginners." Yet you have no idea what you are looking at, what a master-piece that is and the power of Spirit that can work through you in relationship to it.

Your mind does not know anything. Only Knowledge knows. Your personal mind has beliefs and convictions and fixed ideas, but it does not know anything. It was meant to serve Knowledge, not to replace Knowledge. That is why the true recognition happens at a deeper level. The true commitment arises from a deeper level. The true participation is motivated from a deeper level. The waters of the great oceans are moved at a deeper level.

Therefore, you have an opportunity now to have your greater purpose revealed to you in the face of the Great Waves of change, in the face of the Greater Community and in the face of all the uncertainty and unanswerable questions that they present to you. This is the gift. This is the promise. This is the doorway through which you must now pass.

CHAPTER 13

$\mathscr{A}$ New Message of Hope

THERE ARE GREAT WAVES OF CHANGE coming to the world.
They will be unlike anything humanity as a whole has ever had
to face before. They are largely the consequence of humanity's
misuse and overuse of the world and its resources. But they also
represent a real threshold, an evolutionary threshold that
humanity has reached, particularly regarding its encounter with
intelligent life from beyond the world. It will be a time when a
great decision must be made as to whether humanity will unite
and cooperate to share and manage the resources of the world
or whether it will fight and compete, propelling humanity into a
state of constant conflict and permanent decline.

It is a great threshold for individuals as well, whether they
will fight and struggle to preserve what they have or whether
they will unite with others to share and manage the resources
that are available and take responsibility for providing for
those who will not have the basic necessities of life. This is a
practical, physical threshold, and it is a moral and ethical
threshold.

It is likely that humanity will undertake both of these
options until a greater decision can be made and formulated. It
is certain that many things will fail. Communities and even
certain nations may collapse. It is certain that many people will
have to migrate, and there will be a great shift in the order and
function of civilization.

What has been the emphasis in this teaching on the Great

Waves is the great shift that must occur within the individual to recognize the Great Waves of change and to undergo the various steps of preparation that are necessary to approach this great threshold with wisdom and certainty and with the power of Knowledge.

There are many practical things that must be accomplished, of course, and this will draw upon all of the skills and professions of humanity. But if there is no wisdom, if there is no clarity, if there is no deeper incentive to serve others and if there is no ability to adapt to changing and demanding circumstances, then all of the practical skills of humanity, all of the professions of humanity and all of the learned wisdom of humanity will not be sufficient to bring about a greater and more significant outcome.

Every week, every month and every year now is significant, for the Great Waves are moving relentlessly.

It is what the person will see, know and do that will make all the difference in their well-being in the future and in the impact it will have on other people and upon society at large.

The New Message is here to provide a warning, a blessing and a preparation. The warning is now being sounded around the world from many sources, but the severity of the situation is not being recognized by many.

The nature of this great series of changes is being greatly underestimated. People are regarding it as just one of many problems that humanity must face, and they have great confidence that political and technological innovation will take care of the situation or that economic forces will create the necessary adjustments. These assumptions give warning that humanity is underestimating the power of the Great Waves of change.

The fact is that very few people are even aware of the extraterrestrial presence in the world, and even amongst them, very few recognize it as an intervention, as a danger and a hazard for humanity. What this means is that not enough people are aware of the reality of the Great Waves of change and the great impact it will have upon the human family and the future of humanity in this world.

Therefore, God has sent a warning, a blessing and a preparation because time is of the essence. Every week, every month and every year now is significant, for the Great Waves are moving relentlessly. The time it takes to prepare for this is significant, and that window of opportunity is shrinking.

This, therefore, is not something for you to just think about, to contemplate or to simply discuss with your friends, to be a source of imagination or to be simply a source of anxiety and concern. It must propel you into real action. Your awareness must bring about action, and this will require you to consider every aspect of your life and the possibilities that exist in your immediate surroundings and for your nation as a whole. This is not something for the faint of heart, for the ambivalent or for the self-serving, for they will not see the Great Waves of change until it is too late.

This is not something for the faint of heart, for the ambivalent or for the self-serving, for they will not see the Great Waves of change until it is too late.

This is a calling to become aware, to become prepared, to become strong and capable and to begin to take the many steps that will be required to secure your position in the world—to gain a stronger position, to prepare yourself for the shocks that will come and to put yourself in a position to be of service to others, for great service will be needed.

Do not think that the end has come for humanity, that these are the "end times" as some people believe. This is a great turning point. Many things will end. Many attitudes will end. A great part of your conventional thinking will end. Many human activities will end or be diminished. So in that sense, it is the end times.

It is time for humanity to grow up and to cease its desperate struggles and its adolescent indulgences. For you are now emerging into a Greater Community of intelligent life, where humanity must be strong and united, self-sufficient and very discreet. It is a time for humanity to gain a greater maturity as a whole and to take responsibility for managing the world in such a way that it will continue to sustain you into the future and provide what you need in order to live and to advance.

Do not think that the end has come for humanity, that these are the "end times" as some people believe. This is a great turning point.

People have no sense of what this means and its great significance. The consequences of humanity's overuse and misuse of the world are only now beginning to be felt amongst the poorest people of the world. They will be the first to suffer, but the impact of this will reach into every nation and every culture and will affect eventually every person in ways that are tremendous and significant.

This Teaching that you are receiving is not to frighten you into action. It is not to overwhelm you. It is not to diminish you. It is not to discourage you. But you must face reality. You must be prepared and given forewarning of what is coming over the horizon. For if you do not look, you will not see. If you do not see, you will not know. If you do not know, you will not prepare. And if you do not prepare, your life will be in great danger.

That is why there is a New Message from God in the world. It is here to warn you, to strengthen you and to prepare you for the Great Waves of change and for the reality of the Greater Community and all of its challenges and opportunities for humanity.

The New Message is also here to strengthen the individual, to teach people about spirituality at the level of Knowledge, to bring a unifying presence and teaching to all the world's religions, to strengthen human relationships, human families, human commitments and human contribution. It represents a very rare intervention by God for the protection and advancement of humanity. It is a very great Teaching and a great Revelation. Do not think that you can understand it standing apart from it, for you must receive it and bring it into your life, use and apply its wisdom and bring its specific teachings to bear. Only then will you know the power and efficacy of the New Message. And only then will you realize what a blessing it is and how it has come at just the right time.

As it has been said through these Teachings, humanity will enter a period of great confusion and difficulty. It is necessary for you to gain a greater clarity and certainty from the deeper well of Knowledge within you, or you will fall prey to the confusion and the anxiety, the conflict and the hostility that will be arising around you.

You are being given this now as a blessing—the blessing of awareness, the blessing of wisdom and the blessing of having time to prepare yourself, your life, your understanding, your family, your relationships and your circumstances. Time is critical. You must act and act soon if you are to have time to make the necessary adjustments in your life, which within themselves will require time, concentration and many changes.

You must be prepared and given forewarning of what is coming over the horizon.

Do not think that God will save humanity in the end if humanity should choose a path of self-destruction. Do not think that God

will save humanity by removing all the dangers and consequences that have been produced by humanity's ignorance,
arrogance and conflict. Do not think that the innocent will be
spared when the Great Waves of change overtake them.

God has given you the power of Knowledge. God has sent
great emissaries into the world through the course of human
history. God's Angels watch over humanity. God has many
powerful forces in the world influencing individuals, guiding
them and supporting them. There are tremendous powers and
presences here of great benefit to humanity, serving God and
God's great Plan.

Yet the world is a place where humanity must choose, make
its decisions and face the consequences of its decisions. This is a
world apart, where the separated have chosen to live apart
from God, have chosen to create their own reality and have
chosen to take a form of individuality far beyond the distinc-
tions that God has created for each soul. This is a place of
decision. It is a place of contrast. It is a place that is different
from your Ancient Home, from which you have come and to
which you will ultimately return.

Within this environment, there is beauty and there is
ugliness. There is pleasure and there is pain. There are
opportunities and there are dangers. It requires strength and
wisdom to be here and compassion as well if you wish to
experience life and the meaning of a greater purpose here.

Into this difficult learning environment, God has sent a
New Message for humanity, a Message to give humanity a
great chance and a promise for a new beginning—for humanity
to build a greater foundation in the world, to endure the Great
Waves of change, to use its power to unite humanity, to bring
equanimity and fairness to the distribution of resources and to
secure a more profound and stronger position for the future,
one that can be sustained through time.

The New Message has also been sent to prepare humanity
for the Greater Community, to teach humanity the dangers of

premature Contact, to warn humanity of the Intervention that is occurring in the world today and to provide, partially through humanity's remote allies in the Universe, the wisdom that humanity will need to understand the complexities, difficulties and challenges of life in the Universe. This will provide for humanity what it could not provide for itself to engage with this far more complex and far more powerful environment—an environment to which humanity has not yet adapted, an environment that will require great skill and unity amongst the human family.

The New Message has been sent to raise up the individual and to teach about spirituality at the level of Knowledge. The New Message has been sent to teach that all the religions were initiated by God, that all religions were changed by people, that God has created many pathways of redemption to meet the different needs and temperaments of people living at different times and in different cultures and that humanity should never assume God's will or proclaim that their religion alone is the only religion. For God has created many pathways of redemption. Human ignorance and human arrogance here must be corrected if humanity is to find the strength and the will to unite for its own preservation and for the preservation of this beautiful world that has been given to humanity as its home in the Universe.

It is like climbing a great mountain. You must climb this mountain to gain the perspective that you will need to see things clearly.

It is like climbing a great mountain. You must climb this mountain to gain the perspective that you will need to see things clearly. You start at the bottom where everyone is congregated, and you have to leave them to begin this journey. A few people will journey with you. Along the way you will meet others who are journeying and struggling through the various stages and thresholds that one must pass through to continue up this mountain, which will turn out to be far greater and more challenging than you ever imagined at the outset.

While you are still down in the lowlands, blinded by the trees, you cannot see the nature of your life. You cannot see the relationship of this mountain to everything around it. Your vision will be blocked and obscured by all the conditions of your life.

But as you gain altitude on this mountain, you gain strength and clarity, and your life becomes simpler and more efficient, freeing up energy that you need now to proceed, to build a new foundation for yourself and, symbolically, to be able to proceed up this mountain with as little burden and resistance as possible.

You will need to reach a vantage point where you can see clearly the land surrounding you, the circumstances of your life and the greater circumstances of the world—circumstances that you cannot afford now to avoid or to deny, circumstances that you cannot hide from or seek escape from, circumstances that will determine your future and circumstances that can call out of you the greater gifts that God has sent you into the world to give.

This will require a tremendous shift in you, a shift that will happen gradually, a great turning of your life from one of selfish indulgence and fearful attitudes to one of greater strength and objectivity and greater service to others.

Fulfillment is to be found in fulfilling your greater purpose and mission in the world. This kind of fulfillment cannot be found by the acquisition of pleasure, acquisition of things or acquisition of people. Even freedom from pain or freedom from difficulty cannot give you this fulfillment. For it is the fulfillment of the soul; it is fulfilling the deeper needs of the soul. It will take great events to bring this out of you, and great events are now upon you and upon the entire world.

Receive God's New Message. Do not judge it or condemn it. Do not think it is something else. Do not think you can understand it. You have no idea of its power, efficacy or the great range of its teaching. For it is bringing into the world Knowledge and wisdom that have never been brought here before, particularly regarding the Greater Community and the future and the destiny of humanity.

This will all provide you a greater context and a greater level of understanding, which can inform your actions, clarify your ideas and give you a clearer view of what is to come, the journey that you must take and the great service you can provide to others.

There will be other prescriptions for humanity and other prophecies given by various people. But this is the New Message from God. You do not have to believe this and accept this at the outset, but it is very important that you receive its wisdom, that you take advantage of its great teaching, that you receive its gifts of insight and that you put it to use in the world. Belief here is not important. What is important is to receive the gift and to bring it into application in your life and to provide it as a service to others. Only then will you understand the nature of this Revelation. Only then will you know who has created it.

You cannot know God if you stand apart from God. You cannot know God if you stand apart and try to judge and evaluate God or God's work in the world. But you can receive the power and the presence this gives you. And in time you will see that above all things, it is of the greatest importance.

You will have to counteract fear within yourself and within other people. Do not condemn yourself for being afraid, for it is natural. It is normal. It is to be expected. How could you not look at the Great Waves of change and not feel immensely threatened and disconcerted by them? But this reaction, however normal, cannot be your overall response. You must move beyond fear and apprehension to gain a greater strength and objectivity and a greater commitment. You must move out of the pathetic viewpoint of your personal mind and anchor

Knowledge within you is prepared for what is to come and has been preparing you all along.

yourself in a deeper intelligence within yourself that is not afraid of the future, that is not afraid of whatever might come.

This is the great strength that the New Message reveals to you. For why would a difficult future be revealed if this greater strength were not revealed in order to face it and to counteract it? Great times call for great strength. Great events create great individuals and great relationships. The greatness that you carry will never arise under casual or normal circumstances. It must be called out of you by great events and great needs. It must require you to do things that you would be too lazy or indolent to do previously. It must force you to look at the world objectively. It must force you to prepare for a future that you cannot even see at this moment.

This brings the real possibility for fulfillment of the soul to you who have come into the world to face the Great Waves of change, to live at this time of disruption and this time of gravity and opportunity. It is not an accident that you are here at this time. Knowledge within you is prepared for what is to come and has been preparing you all along to face the great thresholds that are now upon the world.

This Teaching is not just for your intellect. It is not just to provide understanding and perspective. It is to ignite a deeper spiritual power within you and a deeper commitment—the deeper commitment that has brought you into the world. This Teaching and this Revelation are not meant to simply create material for you to discuss with your friends, to speculate upon or to argue and debate. If that is all you do with it, you will have missed its great gift. You will have not understood its purpose and its intent.

This is to ignite a deeper commitment. This is to resonate with Knowledge within you who have come into the world to give, who have come into the world to be in the world at this time under these circumstances. This goes beyond your notions about yourself—your identity, how you explain yourself, your circumstances, your name, your appearance, your interests, your hobbies, your relationships and everything.

This speaks of your deeper nature—your deeper and greater reality. For Heaven will not be found in the world. It must be brought here. It must be demonstrated through the giving of people and through authentic relationships and genuine service to the world. This is how Heaven is brought to Earth. This is your greater responsibility. The world now is giving you the greatest opportunity for its realization and its expression.

CHAPTER 14

Seeing, Knowing and Taking Action

To be aware of a great need or a great event represents but the first threshold. To fulfill one's awareness, one must take action. Action is necessary here to bring to fruition one's awareness and to realize one's strength.

There are people who are becoming aware of the Great Waves of change, but who are not taking action regarding them. As a result, they are losing their self-confidence and are not beginning their preparation. Depression, cynicism, ambivalence—these are all the result of not taking action around things that one recognizes to be important. The awareness was not fulfilled, and, as a result, it becomes dark. It becomes clouded, and the inspiration is lost.

Action is necessary to fulfill what one is seeing and knowing. Action does not have to be immediate, however, for there should be a period of contemplation. There are, in fact, three stages in the process of seeing, knowing and acting.

There is seeing a sign. Something stimulates you. You recognize something must be done. There is a time to contemplate, a time of knowing what this is, feeling the need to take it into your mind and your heart. Then there is a time of action. The action itself may have many stages. It may be a very long process, in fact, and that is true within the context of the Great Waves of change. Even a specific change that must

People want to have certainty before they act, but it is the action itself that creates the certainty.

be undertaken in one's life may have many steps involved. You may only know the first few, but it is necessary to move with Knowledge. Only then will you know if what you are seeing is true. Only then will you know its great importance for your life.

People want to have certainty before they act, but it is the action itself that creates the certainty. It is the courage to move and to change one's thinking and one's circumstances that creates the certainty. This is the confirmation. People want to have no doubts before they act. But it is the action itself, if it is true and appropriate, that relieves you from doubt at last.

Knowledge is not in doubt, and if your connection to Knowledge is strong enough, it will carry you beyond the initial resistance, fear, doubt and endless evaluation. For there comes a time to act, and this represents a threshold within itself.

There are many, many people who have known things for a long time. They say to themselves, "I know I must give this up" or "I know I must change this" or "I know I must do this." But they have not yet acted because Knowledge within them is not strong enough yet to overcome their initial resistance.

It is a fact in human nature that people adapt to their circumstances. Even if the circumstances are very compromised, even if the circumstances are very bad, people adapt. This adaptation represents both a strength and a weakness. The fact that humanity can adapt to changing circumstances has given it its great strength and dominance within the world. But the reality that people adapt to situations that are unhealthy for them or that are not in their best interests represents the frailty of human awareness and the degree to which people can compromise themselves to their great detriment.

That is why there is an initial resistance. People have

adapted to something, and change is upsetting. It is costly. It is risky. Unless the situation is utterly terrible, people adapt and build their lives around a set of circumstances. To change requires a great force from within them. This involves inconvenience. It involves self-doubt. It involves living with questions that one cannot fully answer. It involves taking action and giving up privileges or seeming benefits at the outset. For most people adapt to situations that are unhealthy for them because there are certain benefits. Obviously, one must give up those benefits to change those circumstances. Yet this is a small price to pay to relieve oneself of an unhealthy and unhappy situation.

Therefore, there are three stages in knowing something: seeing, knowing and acting. The knowing aspect of this, the second part of this process, involves a deeper resonance and self-inquiry. One must ask, "Is this the truth? Must I take action regarding this?" You can even take a position against what you are seeing to see what kind of response occurs within you. You may test it in this way. You may challenge it. But in the end, if it is true, you will see there is a great certainty that action must be taken regarding that which you see and know.

Once this is recognized, the sooner you take action, the better. Only in rare circumstances does waiting offer any benefit at all. Most people are far overdue in taking action regarding things that they have seen and known. They are afraid to face the discomfort, afraid to face the self-doubt and afraid to give up some small perceived benefit in order to change their attitude or behavior in a way that is utterly beneficial to them.

Clearly, it is not intelligent to pay a great price for a small pleasure, to make a great sacrifice

People adapt and build their lives around a set of circumstances. To change requires a great force from within them.

for a very small reward. Clearly, that is not intelligent. But that is what people do. They make a great sacrifice for a very small reward. They compromise their lives for very, very small seeming advantages. They pay a great price for a very small pleasure. It is the unwillingness to do this that represents a turning point in their lives.

Most people are far overdue in taking action regarding things that they have seen and known.

In the context of preparing for the Great Waves of change, the benefits that you will hold onto are so insignificant compared to the requirements placed upon you that to cling to these benefits represents a kind of self-betrayal. It is as if you have given over your life to some kind of dark force for some small pleasure or advantage. Here there is no escape from self-conflict. Here you cannot really relieve yourself of the problem, for once you have seen and known the truth, you cannot shake this off with all kinds of excuses and justifications.

These three stages all represent conscious acts: seeing, knowing, taking action. Most people will not look, so they will not see. They will not look, they will not really consider what they are seeing, so they look and do not see.

The second error is that people will not be with what they see. They will either dismiss it or give it some kind of simple explanation and file it away somewhere within themselves. They will not keep it in front of them, looking at it. It passes them by. They will not be with it and see what it arouses within themselves, to really examine it and examine their own response to it.

The third stage is taking action, and here again, people do not act. They say, "Ah, I must lose weight" or "I must stop eating this food" or "I must change my work" or "I must fortify my home" or "I must deal with my conflicts in this relationship" or "I must tell this person the thing I must tell them." But they do not act, and so they are stuck. Trying to protect themselves or hold onto some advantage or pleasure, they now put themselves in jeopardy. They sacrifice their awareness, their sense of well-being and their sense of integrity. They are paying immense prices for some small, perceived pleasure or advantage. They are paying huge prices. This is not intelligent. Would you pay $10,000 for a piece of bread or a piece of candy or a little thrill or to avoid an inconvenience or a discomfort? To pay a large sum of money to do this would not be intelligent. You can see this. It is so clear.

So one must be willing to look, to really look at something, to really look at the Great Waves of change—to read about them, to investigate them, to see what they are, to learn more about the Great Waves and how they are affecting people in the world today and their potential for altering the course of human history. What are the implications? People have studied this. Intelligent people have looked at this and are warning others. What is the meaning of this? What are its implications? How could it alter your life and the lives of other people?

Then there is being with what you know and have seen. "What does this really mean for me? Is this really true? And what must I do?"

Then there is taking action—beginning to move, picking yourself up, setting yourself on the road again, regaining your strength, expressing your self-determination and exercising your power and authority. Here you are governing the mind instead of being governed by it. Here you are directing your emotions instead of being directed by them. Here you are overcoming your inertia, overcoming your resistance, while you are gaining self-determination. All these three stages are powerful. They all restore to you your strength, your vision, your capabilities and your sense of direction in life.

So many people do not have a sense of direction because they are not seeing, knowing and acting. They are just going through the motions of life. They are fulfilling social functions. They are doing what their culture tells them to do or what their family expects them to do. They are going through the motions. They are not really seeing very much, they are not really being with what they see sufficiently, and they are not taking action regarding those things that they see and know. And as a result, they are listless, being swept along in the current of what everyone else is doing.

The excuses for this are many, but they all lead to the same kind of self-betrayal. They all weaken you and disconnect you from Knowledge within yourself, Knowledge which is already giving you signs and confirmation. You lose the inspiration if you do not act. Action is necessary.

Here you are governing the mind instead of being governed by it.

In facing the Great Waves of change, you do not have much time. This is both a hazard and an advantage. It is a hazard because if you do not take action soon and begin to reconsider your life, to alter your circumstances and to set in train change that must occur both within your own thinking and emotions and your outer circumstances, you will be at a great disadvantage. For the Great Waves are moving and are already impacting the world and are gaining strength every day.

The advantage in this is that it calls you into action now. It requires that you look and see, that you be with what you see and that you take action regarding it. This inspires action and determination. You do not have time to think about it for very long. You do not have time to vacillate. You do not have time to become ambivalent.

Time is of the essence. If you are feeling the presence of the Great Waves and feel anxiety regarding them, then you are also feeling the anxiety regarding time. How are you spending your time? The discomfort that attends one when one is not responding is significant. And the fact that you do not have much time gives impetus for you to respond and to act.

It takes time to change one's thinking and one's circumstances. It takes time, planning and consideration to alter one's outer circumstances or to change one's relationship with certain people. These things all take time. In many cases, they can be difficult because of the attachments that have been created and the lack of confidence that one has in oneself.

If you wait, then your freedom to respond becomes limited, your options become limited, and you are forced to take dramatic and often drastic actions, which may not be beneficial for you. You do not want to wait until the eleventh hour, for then you will have no options. Your circumstances will be dictated for you, and not by you. Having made no real preparation, you will have to yield to the demands of your situation. This is a position that has few advantages and often great hazards.

Every act of courage and integrity requires overcoming something, releasing something and escaping something.

People wait to take action. They wait too long and then either they cannot take the action that would be most beneficial or they must pay a great price for doing it, far greater than they would have had to pay initially.

It is true, you must earn your freedom. It is not free. Every act of courage and integrity requires overcoming something, releasing something and escaping something, both within yourself and outside of yourself. Life is moving. You must move with it. You must prepare for it, you must respond to it, you must feel it and experience it, and you must take action.

The "Recommendations for Living in a Great Waves World" provides a set of questions and directives that apply to nearly everyone. This is the beginning preparation for the Great

Waves of change. It is the beginning because the Great Waves will be long lasting, and there is no set of written guidelines that can answer everyone's needs and questions. Beyond fulfilling the "Recommendations" and using them fully, one must rely upon Knowledge and the wisdom one possesses and the wisdom of others to make wise decisions. Because everyone's life is different—their circumstances, their obligations, their relationships and the state of their own mental and physical health—their pathways are all different. That is why one prescription will not work for everyone.

It is to bring you to the great guidance of Knowledge ultimately that will give you the strength and the wisdom you need to proceed. But certain initial preparations must be made. If your circumstances are putting you in great jeopardy in the face of the Great Waves of change, you must attend to them now. Do not wait, or you may not be able to change them.

Where you live, how you live, how you move about, your work, your health, the amount of support you gain from your relationships, your behavior and your emotions—these are all very important. It is not enough to just change one's thinking. One must change one's life.

Here you will have to override your social conditioning and your weaker tendencies—disappointing other people, breaking the chains that hold you in place. The power to do this comes from your determination not to be a slave to other forces, not to be bound and hindered by things that are not true and genuine. You build the strength to do this by doing this. This is what will carry you forward.

The New Message will provide the tools, but you must use them and learn to use them wisely—building the Four Pillars of your life to counteract eccentricity in areas of your life where you are in denial; building a solid foundation; building a strong relationship with yourself, with other people, with where you live, with what you do, with how you think; discovering your strengths and your weaknesses, fortifying the former and managing the latter. There is no other way if you are to become strong and self-determined in the face of the Great Waves of change.

There is no safety and security now to hide behind or to relinquish your strength to. For what security will there be in pretending that there is not a great challenge, holding onto what little you have, attaching yourself to whatever gives you a temporary sense of security and well-being? What security will there be? What will not be challenged? What will not be vulnerable to the Great Waves of change?

Life is giving you signs. It is telling you what is coming. Knowledge within you is giving you signs, urging you to respond.

Many people will go down with the ship because they do not want to leave the ship, while others have escaped, waiting to be rescued. This is the sad truth about human existence because humanity as a whole has not really become strong and united sufficiently. But individuals have and always have, and now many more must gain this strength and stability and this focus.

Life is giving you signs. It is telling you what is coming. Knowledge within you is giving you signs, urging you to respond.

People use confusion as a place to hide, to mask the things that they are recognizing and to avoid being with these things and taking action. It is like a smokescreen so that people will not have to see, know and act and take the risks and face the challenge. It is a group addiction. It is a mass avoidance.

The masses of people are living at a very low level of integrity. You cannot allow this for yourself. You must choose otherwise, and if this means you have to leave your friends or break away from your family, this is what it will require. This is what has been required of all the great saints and messengers and all the people who have gone on to do important and great

For there are many voices within you, but only one is true.

things. In nearly all cases, they had to break away from their former allegiances to have the freedom, the strength and the opportunity to assume a greater life and a greater service.

Think not that your life is not important enough to do this. Pay attention to what you tell yourself in this regard. For there are many voices within you, but only one is true. There is the voice of your culture. There is the voice of your family and parents. There is the voice of your friends. There is the voice of your religious tradition, if you have a religious tradition. There is the voice of your teachers and other influential people in your life. Then there is the voice of Knowledge, which speaks through your feelings, through your ideas and through your physical sensations. Ultimately, only one of these voices is true. Knowledge may be reflected in the wisdom of your parents, the wisdom of your friends, the wisdom of your teachers, even the wisdom of your culture, but this wisdom is rare and exceptional.

Take time now to be with this. Stop your endless running around and take time to be with this Greater Community message and to be with the reality of the Great Waves of change. Take retreat. Do not discuss it yet with your friends. You must consider it first within yourself. You must establish your own relationship with it first. Do not bring it into idle conversation. Do not seek the opinions of others until you yourself know the truth for yourself.

This is discretion, and it is important. People give away their certainty through idle conversation with others. This is a calling to you, for you, not for them. They have their own calling. This is your calling. How will you respond to it?

Observe yourself. See what your mind tells you. Listen to the different voices within you. Do you use reason or emotion or the consensus of others or authority figures to dissuade you from being with something that you see? What are the ways that you undermine your certainty and invalidate your own experience? Do you use reason or faith or assumptions or other people's authority or convention or history—what do you use to betray yourself and your experience? You must know this. You must know both your strengths and your weaknesses. You must know your tendencies regarding seeing, knowing and acting.

You will need to moderate your behavior and your thinking. This can be done. You have the power. You are not simply a slave to your feelings or to your social conditioning. You have the power. But to know this power, you must use it, and you must act upon it. Otherwise, power is just an idea, a fleeting moment of experience, a recognition but not yet a functioning reality within you.

The Great Waves have everything to do with who you are and why you are in the world. But how will you know this unless you become engaged, unless you take action, unless you commit yourself to taking this action? Relationship is realized through recognition, through resonance and through taking action. This is true with your relationship with a person, with a place or with a great set of events.

You cannot sit on the sidelines and understand. You will never see the truth there. You must enter the fray because this is your life. This is why you have come. This has everything to do with your circumstances, with your well-being, with your freedom, with the value and quality of your life and with the value and quality of your most precious relationships.

This is why God has given you Knowledge—to guide you, to protect you and to lead you into a greater life. This is why Knowledge

You cannot sit on the sidelines and understand. You will never see the truth there. You must enter the fray because this is your life.

Events will happen whether you are ready or not. You cannot wish them away.

holds the key to whether you will respond to the Great Waves and to the wisdom, the meaning and the value of your response.

You must be willing to do things that other people are not doing. You must be willing to see things that other people are not seeing, to know things that other people are not knowing and to take action that other people are not taking because in truth you may be the only person you know or one of very few you know who is doing anything to respond and to prepare. This is how Knowledge becomes strong in you.

Human beings are not herds of cattle or herds of sheep though they can behave like this in so many ways. Yet this is not their reality. To gain the strength to respond differently, you must adopt this strength and you must act upon it. There is no other way for you to know its truth and its value for you.

Life now is giving you the perfect motivation to do this. You are no longer living under quiescent circumstances where nothing is demanding anything of you. To the contrary, you are living under evermore demanding circumstances, and life is demanding many things from you. What is the most important thing that life is demanding? To answer this question, look not only within yourself, but also beyond yourself to see what is brewing on the horizon. Events will happen whether you are ready or not. You cannot wish them away. They will happen no matter what your state of mind or state of consciousness.

The Great Waves of change are coming. They are building. They are emerging on the horizon. They are already affecting millions of people around the world. What will you do now? What will you follow? What voice within yourself will you follow? What wisdom beyond yourself will you heed? How much courage will you muster? How far will you go in your preparation? How seriously will you take the situation? To what degree will you compromise yourself to meet the intentions or the expectations of others?

Only you can answer these questions. Here you are being given the gift of awareness. This is a gift that is given with love and with respect. God honors the great strength in you, a great strength that you are only beginning to discover. God honors your greater purpose for being in the world, a greater purpose that you are only beginning to discern and to discover. God is giving you the great advantage of forewarning—a forewarning that will be up to you to discern and to either accept or reject.

This is God's gift to you. And it must be your gift to yourself. It must be your gift to your children, to your friends, to your family and to anyone who has the power and the intelligence to listen.

You must prepare your children, for they will be living in a world of ever greater change and difficulty. You strengthen them not by telling them what is coming, but by strengthening their connection to Knowledge, by teaching them the difference between fantasy and reality, by helping them to discern the nature of their own strengths and weaknesses, by sharing with them the wisdom that you have learned in life and by showing them where they can gain greater wisdom through the experiences of others.

This is an immense gift to your children. But your greatest gift is through demonstration—the integrity and the quality of the life that you determine and that you choose and how you respond to the demands of life. This is the greatest gift to your children. If you are weak and compromised, that is what you will teach them. If you are self-deceiving, that is what you will teach them. If you capitulate to the expectations of others, that is what you will teach them.

> *You must prepare your children, for they will be living in a world of ever greater change and difficulty.*

Focus on those who can respond and not on those who cannot respond.

Yet if you truly can see, if you truly can know and can truly take action, this is what you will teach them. If you recognize that life is changing and moving and that you must change and move with it, that is what you will teach them. If you can experience the power and the presence of Knowledge within yourself and express this and act upon this, that is what you will teach them. They are looking to you to teach them either wisdom or folly, self-respect or self-deception. You are a leader in this regard.

There are other people in your life who are looking to you also, to see what you can teach them. It is your demonstration born of Knowledge, born of wisdom, born of seeing, knowing and acting that will be the inspiration that you give to others, and this inspiration will be immensely important.

The Creator of all life loves humanity and has given humanity the power and the presence of Knowledge and has given humanity an Angelic Presence to oversee the world and to provide guidance and counsel to those who are beginning to respond to the presence of Knowledge within themselves. You cannot understand this intellectually, but it is already part of your experience.

You must put your faith in the strength that God has put within you and in the strength and integrity that God has put within others. Focus on those who can respond and not on those who cannot respond. Give to those who can receive the gift and share it with others. Encourage those who are responding instead of trying to persuade those who cannot or will not respond. Gather around you those who are strong and who see the need to become strong. Do not spend time and energy trying to persuade someone who cannot or will not respond. That will only waste your vitality, which must be brought to bear now.

Humanity will be led by those who are strong with Knowledge and by those who recognize the importance of their integrity and the value of their true relationships. Everyone who can do this is a leader—within their families, within their circle of friends and influence, even within the leadership of those in religion and government.

Your task now is to prepare and to become strong with Knowledge. Do not take your eyes off this task. Do not become overly concerned with other people. Do not become disheartened at the lack of response in people around you. You must bring all of your attention to bear on what you yourself must do. It will take all of your strength to do this.

Do not complain about the world. Do not be overly critical of other people, for in the face of the Great Waves of change, many people will increase their foolishness and their self-deception. They will act even more foolishly. But you must bring your attention to bear on what is before you to see, to know and to do. If others are sinking, you must rise. If others are failing, you must succeed.

This then will be your gift to others. You will give others this strength as you gain it yourself. This begins to fulfill a greater purpose and a greater destiny that you have for being in the world. For there is your specific contribution, which remains to be discovered, and then there is the power and the presence of Knowledge. Receive this power, express this power and encourage this power in others. Teach your children the power and the presence of Knowledge within themselves and the great dangers of self-deception and social manipulation.

If you can do this, you will see that the Great Waves of change, though extremely hazardous and consequential, in fact represent a great calling. It is a great calling for Knowledge to emerge and a great calling for people to respond

You must bring all of your attention to bear on what you yourself must do.

and to become strong and united—to cease their endless conflicts with one another, to unite to protect the world, to preserve what is great in the human family and to lay the foundation for a greater future and a new direction, a new way forward for humanity.

These are the great times in which you live. They call for the greatness that you have brought into the world from your Ancient Home—a power and a presence which you must now experience for yourself.

Important Terms

THE GREAT WAVES OF CHANGE: The powerful set of converging forces that will dramatically alter our environment, climate, resources and economic reality, affecting every aspect of our lives and the future of our world.

KNOWLEDGE: The deeper spiritual intelligence that lives within each person. This intelligence exists beyond the realm of the intellect and is the source of all that we know. Intrinsic understanding. Eternal wisdom to guide us, to protect us and to lead us to a greater participation in life. Knowledge is the timeless part of us which cannot be influenced, manipulated or corrupted.

THE WAY OF KNOWLEDGE: The most essential spiritual teaching there is. The foundation of all the world's religions. The greatest promise for humanity and now the greatest need for humanity. Any progress that any person can make in learning the Way of Knowledge further assures humanity's well-being in the future. The emphasis here is not on enlightenment. The emphasis is on being grounded in Knowledge—sober, clear, observant, ready to respond and ready to give what you know you must give wherever your gift is meant to be given.

STEPS TO KNOWLEDGE: *Steps to Knowledge* is the New Message book of spiritual practice. Presented in a self-study format, it contains 365 Steps that enable you to experience inner certainty and direction. It is this experience that can sustain

and guide you every day and in every situation. It is the
map and guidebook that you will take with you into the
Great Waves.

GOD: God is the Source of Knowledge within you, Knowledge
being the deeper spiritual mind that the Creator has
bestowed upon you and upon all sentient beings in the
Universe. God has created the diversity of life in the
physical Universe and has set in motion an evolutionary
process to occupy all space and time.

NEW MESSAGE FROM GOD: The New Message from God is a
genuine communication from the Creator that has been sent
into the world at a time of great change, conflict and
upheaval. The New Message provides the knowledge,
wisdom and direction that humanity could not provide for
itself to meet the great challenges that are now facing the
entire human family. The New Message is not based upon
any existing religious tradition or spiritual teaching. It is a
gift for people of all nations and faiths. It honors the
enduring truth in all the great Messages that the Creator
has ever given to the world, yet it is unlike anything that
has ever been revealed to humanity before.

THE GREATER COMMUNITY: Space. The vast physical Universe
into which humanity is emerging, which contains intelligent
life in countless manifestations and stages of evolution. The
Greater Community is a competitive environment on a vast
and incomprehensible scale. It represents the greatest
threshold humanity will ever face, but we are unprepared.

HUMAN DESTINY: It is the destiny of all peoples living in the
world today to face the Great Waves of change and
humanity's encounter with intelligent life from the Greater
Community. This is our evolution. It is our destiny to

emerge into the Greater Community as a free and self-determined race.

SIGNS: Messages from both Knowledge within us and from the world at large, alerting us to dangers, opportunities and changing circumstances. Signs emerging within us can take the form of images, prevailing thoughts, an inner voice, dreams or powerful physical sensations, depending upon our individual nature and orientation.

SEEING: The ability to see above and beyond our fears and preferences in order to recognize the meaning of changing circumstances and the signs of future events coming over the horizon. To have this clarity of mind, you must be watching without coming to conclusions, without trying to tie things together, without trying to make things simple and comprehensible. Instead, like building a puzzle, you allow the pieces to emerge and to fit together. This is called seeing.

THE LOVE/FEAR DICHOTOMY: The belief that there are only two perspectives in viewing ourselves, others and the world: love and fear. The Great Waves teaching disputes this notion as blind, preferential and self-limiting. Real love is not always kind and reassuring. And real fear, as opposed to imaginary fear, is nature's way of alerting you to danger. Anxiety and discomfort are often signs that there is something that needs to be attended to and acted upon in your life. To deny these experiences as being unloving is to deny yourself the reality, the wisdom and the benefits of the full range of your experience in life.

INTELLIGENCE: Real intelligence is the ability and the desire to learn and to adapt. Real intelligence is not simply solving complex problems or being clever and witty. For if you cannot see and you cannot know, what advantage do these aspects of your mind give you? Real intelligence is the ability to see, to know and to act with commitment and certainty guided by Knowledge.

$\mathcal{R}$ecommendations for
Living in a Great Waves World

PRESENTED HERE ARE RECOMMENDATIONS to assist you in beginning to prepare for the Great Waves of change. Since each person's life, circumstances and higher purpose are unique, there is no set of recommendations that can speak to every circumstance and need. Yet these recommendations will be important in helping you to focus your activities and in supporting you on your path of preparation. Please note that these are recommendations, not rules. Use them and adapt them to your circumstances. They are given here to assist you in bringing balance, strength and direction to your life.

PREPARING YOUR OUTER LIFE

- *Conserve energy* as much as possible. Reduce your energy consumption by 25–50% or more to help save your community and the world from depletion and ruin.

- *Maintain a supply of food, water and medicine* to prepare for difficulties ahead—at least a supply for 90 days. If your living space is limited, store whatever amount of supplies that you can.

ᴖ *Build an emergency cash fund*, if possible, to sustain you during economic disruptions or job loss. In light of the Great Waves, take a more active role in managing, directing and building your financial resources.

ᴖ *Consider the availability of medical services* in your area and how they may or may not function in a disaster or in a prolonged emergency. For those with chronic medical conditions, keep an adequate supply of prescription medicine on hand.

ᴖ *Consider learning how to grow some of your own food*. You can do this on your own or together with others.

ᴖ *Own fewer things*. Make sure that everything you own really serves you. Travel light and create time for more important things.

ᴖ *Consider where you live* in light of the Great Waves of change. In your current location, are you able and willing to travel without the use of an automobile? Will you be able to assist others given your current location and circumstances? Will you be ready to help others in times of need, or will you yourself be in jeopardy?

ᴖ *Consider your profession,* and ask yourself these important questions: Will my line of work be sustainable in the years ahead given the constraints on energy, food and other resources? Is my profession or line of work involved with providing essential goods or servicing real needs, or does it involve products or services that are non-essential and that may not be sustained in the difficult times ahead?

ᴖ *Educate others*, including your friends, family, neighbors and coworkers, about the Great Waves of change. The more people around you who are aware, the better prepared your community will be.

◦ *Consider the frail, the elderly and the vulnerable* in your local community or neighborhood. Think ahead of how you might be able to help them if that becomes necessary.

◦ *Support your local merchants, farmers and producers*, for they will be significant resources in the future when the ability to transport goods and services will be far more limited than it is today.

◦ *Learn where your essential resources come from*, how you might be able to acquire them if there were interruptions in supply and what you would do if for any reason they became unavailable.

◦ *Be sensitive and aware of the possibility of natural disasters* in your area that could pose hazards to your safety. Have a contingency plan of what you would do in such an extreme event.

◦ *Inquire into your local town, city or regional government's plans and preparations*, if any, regarding Great Waves scenarios that are likely to emerge in your area. Provide feedback to your representatives and other local officials.

◦ *Build strong personal relationships* that can help you in your preparation. Are those close to you responding to the Great Waves of change, or do you find yourself having to persuade and convince them, often without success?

◦ *Continue to educate yourself about the Great Waves of change* as they unfold in the world. Use caution and discernment when considering the opinions of others and the commentary of experts.

PREPARING YOUR INNER LIFE

∾ *Take quiet time each day* to consider the wisdom of your thoughts and actions and to become aware of any insights you have had. Keep a journal of these insights and review them frequently.

∾ *Adopt a simple meditation practice* to relieve stress and to connect to Knowledge, the deeper intelligence within you. The study in *Steps to Knowledge* provides a pathway for doing this.

∾ *Have few opinions.* Make no opinions about any problem unless you have spent considerable time studying the problem and its many conceived interpretations and solutions. Ask yourself if you are really certain about something or are only guessing.

∾ *Stop complaining.* Do not waste your precious time and energy complaining about something if you are not prepared to take action regarding it. Instead use your time and energy, your thoughts and resources, to prepare yourself, to prepare others and to strengthen your connection to Knowledge.

∾ *Reassess your goals and plans* to see if these are really going to be possible in a radically changing world. Ask yourself, "In a world of diminishing resources, environmental degradation and economic hardship, are my plans and goals practical and viable, given these circumstances?" You will begin to feel the truth about this.

∾ *Forgive others.* Forgive those who seem to err against you and the world. Ask yourself what genuine need they are attempting to express and fulfill by their behavior. Practicing forgiveness will save your emotional energy and keep your mind clear.

∾ *Honor your parents,* and try to understand the circumstances of their lives that determined their decisions and behavior.

∾ *Forgive yourself.* Learn from your own errors, and recognize and use the wisdom that they have provided to you. Knowing your past mistakes and learning from them will help you in facing and navigating the Great Waves of change. If you don't forgive yourself, you lose self-trust, which you will need to rely upon increasingly in the future. You build self-trust most powerfully by following Knowledge within you.

∾ *Build and maintain the Four Pillars of your life.* Consider that you have Four Pillars that, like the four legs of a table, are upholding your life:

- The Pillar of Relationships
- The Pillar of Health
- The Pillar of Work and Providership
- The Pillar of Spiritual Development

To be happy, stable and successful, you will need to build and maintain each of these Pillars and not sacrifice one for the others.

∾ *Do not succumb to fear* or believe that you have no power in the face of these great changes, for you have the power of Knowledge within you to guide and protect you if you can follow it. Your experience of Knowledge, or inner knowing, will enable you to set a new direction, evaluate problems clearly and make wise decisions, even if no one else around you is doing this.

∾ *Build self-confidence.* You gain confidence by seeing what is necessary and taking action. You begin by doing small things, everything you can see to do, step by step, to prepare yourself, to prepare your mind, to prepare your circumstances, to prepare your home and to prepare your relationships.

∾ *Be a catalyst for change,* and do not rely upon consensus or agreement from others. Learn to honor the importance of your decisions and how to make these decisions based upon the deeper Knowledge within you. This self-reliance and the strength of Knowledge may well save your life.

∾ *Assess your relationships.* Who has a real destiny with you? Are these the people who are with you now?

∾ *Learn to follow Knowledge,* the deeper spiritual intelligence within you, and to recognize the Great Waves of change that are coming so that you can become informed and prepared in a timely manner. The experience of Knowledge may take the form of an image, a powerful insight or a persistent feeling that does not go away.

∾ *Have great faith in Knowledge* within yourself and within humanity as a whole. Otherwise, the Great Waves will seem overwhelming—too great to consider, too great to prepare for, too great to navigate. And you will simply give up and feel defeated before the real trials begin.

∾ *Recognize that you are entering a time of great challenge and change* in the world and that this challenge and change will make you strong and will call out of you the greater gifts that you have been sent into the world to give. For you have come into the world on a mission, and the reality of that mission is contained within Knowledge, the deeper intelligence within you, waiting to be discovered.

In conclusion, as has been stated many times, the solution to the unfolding planetary issues is, at its core, a spiritual one. Interested readers are encouraged to explore the other books written by MV Summers and published by New Knowledge Library at www.newknowledgelibrary.org.

Great Waves of Change Practices

It is important to use and apply practices that can bring a greater clarity and certainty to your life. The practices below are from the chapters of *The Great Waves of Change* and from other writings by MV Summers. With any practice, it is valuable to practice at regular intervals over time to deepen your experience. These practices build the kind of skills and awareness that you will need to prepare.

There are many practices here to choose from. Each is important. Choose what is most appropriate to your needs and interests at this moment, but do not neglect the others, for they are all important in deepening your connection to Knowledge, the Knowing Mind within you, and in preparing you for the Great Waves of change.

∿ Where to live

Ask yourself, "Where should I live?" Keep asking, and the steps will begin to appear if there is any change you must make in this regard. You cannot ask only once. You must ask repeatedly. You must be with the question. You must live with the question and be open, really open, to what might be presented to you, particularly if you already sense that where you are is not permanent, or you have concern over its viability as a place to live in the future.

CHAPTER 2: THE GREAT WAVES AND YOUR LIFE

◦ *Recognizing the signs*

To begin, you must learn to become still and observant—looking without judging, looking without coming to conclusions, looking for signs. The signs are not everywhere, but they are abundant enough that if you are observant and give yourself to being observant as you pass through your day, then you will begin to see things, and they will stand out from everything else. They will stand out. They will impress you more than just the usual kinds of fascinating things or disturbing things you may hear about or read about. They will impress you at a deeper level. Pay attention. Write them down. Keep a record of them with a date and a time and a place so you can begin to bring the pieces of the puzzle together.

CHAPTER 4: THE FREEDOM TO MOVE WITH KNOWLEDGE

◦ *Where you are now*

The great evaluation begins with taking stock of where you are now—how you spend your time, your energy, your focus and your interests.

- Where is your life being given away?
- What is it being focused upon?
- Where is it being assigned?

You only have so much energy in the day, so much time in the day and so much space within your mind to consider things.

- Where is that all going now?
- What are you doing?
- What are your priorities?
- Where are you gaining energy in your life, and where are you losing it?

- To whom are you losing it, or to what are you losing it?
- Where do you feel certainty, and where do you feel uncertain?
- What relationships are you in now that give you a sense of certainty and direction?
- Which relationships cloud that certainty or obstruct it completely?
- Where are you right now?
- Who are you with, and what are you doing with them?
- What do you own, and is it giving you strength or taking strength away from you?
- What do you believe, and are your beliefs giving you clarity, or are they a replacement for Knowledge itself?
- Where is your time going?
- If you sit in meditation, what is concerning your mind?
- Where is your mind going, and what problems is it solving?

CHAPTER 5: THE DEEP EVALUATION

∿ Possessions

Begin then with simple things. Review everything that you own. Everything that you own, even insignificant things, has a value to you of some kind and in a subtle way represents an influence. If your life is full of things that have no usefulness or purpose, then they are taking time and energy from you to a certain degree. You still own them, and so you are still in relationship with them. They are occupying space in your home and in your mind. Everything you own really either needs to be fundamentally practical and necessary or personally very meaningful, and that meaning must come in a way that supports who you are now and where you feel you are heading in life.

<small>CHAPTER 5: THE DEEP EVALUATION</small>

∾ Sorting out possessions

The process is one of sorting out, bringing a greater objectivity into your life—looking at every possession that you have and asking, "Is this really useful to me? Is it personally meaningful to me? And does it enhance and strengthen my awareness and understanding of myself?"

<small>CHAPTER 5: THE DEEP EVALUATION</small>

∾ Relationships

Regarding relationships that you choose and select for yourself, you must evaluate each one: "Is this relationship strengthening me or weakening me? Is this person moving in the direction that I must move? Do we have a greater destiny together, or should I release this person to follow their own journey in life?"

<small>CHAPTER 5: THE DEEP EVALUATION</small>

∾ Evaluating discomfort

The truth is you are not where you need to be in life, and you know this, and that is why you are uncomfortable. Do not try to get rid of the discomfort, for it is a sign within you that your life must move, that there is change that must be brought about, and that you must do it. Allow yourself to be with the discomfort. Feel it. See what it is telling you. See where it is taking you. Where are the points of discomfort? Where is the lie being lived in your life? What are the mistruths you are telling yourself about your relationship with this person, this place or this thing?

CHAPTER 5: THE DEEP EVALUATION

∿ *What to watch for in the world*

- You must become aware of situations around the world regarding the availability of food and water.

- You must become aware of changes in climate and its effects upon food production in the world and its effects upon the well-being of people in both urban and rural environments.

- You must be aware of political and economic instability and how it is manifesting within certain places.

- You must be aware of any outbreaks of pandemic illness.

- You must be aware of conflicts that continue to exist and conflicts that may emerge in the future. When you look at the world, look for these things. Just bear witness to them and see if there are any signs. Not everything you will look at is important. Not everything you look at will be a sign.

CHAPTER 6: RELATIONSHIPS AND THE GREAT WAVES

∿ *Doing what you know*

Ask yourself, "What must I do now in order to prepare myself and my family?" Already there are things you know you must do. Perhaps you have known them for some time. You must do them now. Do the things you know you must do today, and tomorrow you will know other things that you must do. If you do them, you will know more things that you must do. It is by doing that you gain greater clarity. Completing the tasks you know you must do shows you the other tasks that must be completed.

CHAPTER 7: PREPARING YOUR FAMILY

✎ Assets and liabilities

You must think of these things now—not emotionally, but reasonably—considering your advantages and disadvantages based upon where you live, how you live and how you travel about. What assets do you have? What are your liabilities? What is the strength of your position? Do you need to change your living circumstances radically in the face of the Great Waves of change? If so, you will need to do this fairly quickly because these things take time, and time is what you do not have a lot of. If there are shortages of fuel, or if the price of everything escalates beyond what you can afford, what will you do then?

CHAPTER 8: THE DANGER OF ISOLATION

✎ Escaping isolation

You must bridge your isolation. Become involved in your local community. Speak in your local city councils and governments. Find out what your town or your city or your nation is doing to prepare for these great difficulties. Read, become educated, go visit people, participate. Escape your isolation and self-obsession. Become involved. Become an advocate. Share the revelation in this book with other people. Read what other people are discovering as they begin to discern the Great Waves of change. This is healthy for you. It is redemptive for you. It will give you confidence if you act. If you do nothing, your confidence will fall away, and you will sink into despair. Then you will be truly powerless and truly vulnerable.

CHAPTER 8: THE DANGER OF ISOLATION

∾ Dangerous places to live

If you live in a desert region of the nation, you may have to leave, as there may be no water for you in the future, and it may be very difficult for food to reach your community. Do not live near moving water, near rivers that will overflow in the face of violent weather and changing climate conditions. It is wise to move away from coastal regions that will be affected by violent weather and in many cases from certain large cities that will be subject to extreme social unrest.

CHAPTER 8: THE DANGER OF ISOLATION

∾ How Knowledge speaks to you

Knowledge will speak to you through your thoughts, through your feelings. But it will not speak through fear, it will not speak through fantasy, and it will not speak to your preferences. You must be open, asking Knowledge within yourself, "What must I do now? What is the next step for me? How shall I regard this particular situation? What decision should I make regarding this particular thing?"

CHAPTER 8: THE DANGER OF ISOLATION

∾ Bringing questions to Knowledge

Here you must bring everything to Knowledge. Ask Knowledge, "Is this a good idea?" Ask Knowledge, "Should I follow the recommendations of this person?" Perhaps you will feel resistance; perhaps Knowledge will be silent. Both indicate that you should stop and not proceed with that decision or follow that person.

CHAPTER 8: THE DANGER OF ISOLATION

～ *People and community*

Rethink your life—your relationship with where you live, the house you live in, your work, your transportation, your relationships.

– Who is wise amongst those whom you know?

– Who has skills?

– Who is strong?

– Who can face the Great Waves of change?

Learn what the resources of your community are.

– What can they provide?

– What assets do they really have that can support you and your community?

CHAPTER 8: THE DANGER OF ISOLATION

～ *Where to place your faith*

– Your question, then, is where will you place your faith?

– Where is your faith placed even right now?

– What will give you true strength, confidence, courage and determination?

– What will give you the power to overcome your own weaknesses, your own ambition, your own inhibition and your fear of disapproval by others?

– What will give you the power to overcome your social conditioning to meet a greater need and a greater set of problems?

– What will keep you above fear and hopelessness?

CHAPTER 11: WHERE WILL YOU PLACE YOUR FAITH?

∾ *Beginning guidelines*

"Recommendations for Living in a Great Waves World" are really only beginning guidelines because everyone's circumstances will be somewhat different, and everyone has a unique mission and purpose in life to discover and to fulfill. So beyond establishing initial steps and building a basic foundation, you will have to rely upon Knowledge within yourself and Knowledge within others to navigate the changing and uncertain times ahead.

CHAPTER 12: YOUR PURPOSE AND DESTINY IN A CHANGING WORLD

∾ *The importance of inner preparation*

Your inner preparation here is more significant than anything you do on the outside, for whatever you do on the outside is a temporary expedient. You cannot store food for the rest of your life. You cannot protect yourself from every event and eventuality. You cannot stockpile for decades. And there will be no place on Earth that will be entirely safe or beyond the reach of the Great Waves of change.

CHAPTER 12: YOUR PURPOSE AND DESTINY IN A CHANGING WORLD

∾ *Knowing the truth*

There are three stages in knowing something: seeing, knowing and acting. The knowing aspect of this, the second part of this process, involves a deeper resonance and self-inquiry. One must ask, "Is this the truth? Must I take action regarding this?" You can even take a position against what you are seeing to see what kind of response occurs within you. You may test it in this way. You may challenge it. But in the end, if it is true, you will see there is a great certainty that action must be taken regarding that which you see and know.

CHAPTER 14: SEEING, KNOWING AND TAKING ACTION

∾ *Studying the Great Waves of change*

One must be willing to look, to really look at something, to really look at the Great Waves of change—to read about them, to investigate them, to see what they are, to learn more about the Great Waves and how they are affecting people in the world today and their potential for altering the course of human history. What are the implications? People have studied this. Intelligent people have looked at this and are warning others. What is the meaning of this? What are its implications? How could it alter your life and the lives of other people?

CHAPTER 14: SEEING, KNOWING AND TAKING ACTION

∾ *Being with what you know*

Then there is being with what you know and have seen. "What does this really mean for me? Is this really true? And what must I do?"

CHAPTER 14: SEEING, KNOWING AND TAKING ACTION

∾ *What undermines your certainty*

Observe yourself. See what your mind tells you. Listen to the different voices within you. Do you use reason or emotion or the consensus of others or authority figures to dissuade you from being with something that you see? What are the ways that you undermine your certainty and invalidate your own experience? Do you use reason or faith or assumptions or other people's authority or convention or history—what do you use to betray yourself and your experience? You must know this. You must know both your strengths and your weaknesses. You must know your tendencies regarding seeing, knowing and acting.

CHAPTER 14: SEEING, KNOWING AND TAKING ACTION

∿ *What you will follow*

The Great Waves of change are coming. They are building. They are emerging on the horizon. They are already affecting millions of people around the world.

– What will you do now?

– What will you follow?

– What voice within yourself will you follow?

– What wisdom beyond yourself will you heed?

– How much courage will you muster?

– How far will you go in your preparation?

– How seriously will you take the situation?

– To what degree will you compromise yourself to meet the intentions or the expectations of others?

CHAPTER 14: SEEING, KNOWING AND TAKING ACTION

∿ *Preparing your children*

You must prepare your children, for they will be living and entering into a world of ever greater change and difficulty. You strengthen them not by telling them what is coming, but by strengthening their connection to Knowledge, by teaching them the difference between fantasy and reality, by helping them to discern the nature of their own strengths and weaknesses, by sharing with them the wisdom that you have learned in life and by showing them where they can gain greater wisdom through the experiences of others.

CHAPTER 14: SEEING, KNOWING AND TAKING ACTION

There is much more wisdom to be found at
www.greatwavesofchange.org.

STILLNESS MEDITATION PRACTICE

Practicing stillness is essential if you are to experience the deeper movement of your life and to receive the guidance of Knowledge within yourself in preparing for the Great Waves of change. Here you will be going beneath the surface of your mind to experience quieter levels of thought or even no thought at all. This is extremely restful and rejuvenating.

There are four important elements to build a meditation practice of this kind. First, it is important to practice in a quiet place without distractions or interruptions. Dedicate, if possible, a small place in your home for this purpose and enhance that environment to support your practice.

Second, you need to be physically comfortable while you practice. Since you will be sitting for this practice, find a comfortable chair or cushions to support you.

Third, you will need to approach your practice with a passive attitude. This means that you are in a relaxed state of mind, not trying to get anything such as insights or answers. You are moving towards achieving a state of stillness or meditation.

Lastly, you need something to focus your mind on so that it does not constantly wander. You can do this either by following your breath or by uttering silently a meaningless word or sound. If your mind begins to wander to thoughts or memories, gently bring it back to your breath or to the sound that you are using. Whatever happens, just keep bringing your mind back to your breath or your sound. Keep bringing your attention back. Using your breath or this sound will, over time, bring you into the experience of deeper and more subtle levels of the mind, like a pebble sinking into a deep pool. Here you are entering the realm of Knowledge, beyond the reach of the intellect.

Therefore, to begin, take time and go to your dedicated practice space. Turn off your phone and any other devices that could interrupt your practice time. Sit up comfortably in a chair or on the floor. Take a series of deep breaths in order to relax. Close your eyes and begin to focus on either your breathing or upon a word or sound. You can naturally follow your breath or you can utter a word silently. In the study of *Steps to Knowledge*, the sound *Na Rahn* is recommended. Here you say to yourself softly *Na* on the inhale and *Rahn* on the exhale.

Whether you follow your breath or use a sound such as *Na Rahn*, it is important to stay with it. Your mind will tend to wander, calling up images or problems, memories or concerns. As you continue, practicing stillness will become easier, and you will find yourself experiencing a very relaxed, but alert state. If you find initially that you tend to fall asleep, this is all right. It just means that you may have a pronounced need for rest. Eventually you will not fall asleep, but instead, achieve a state of meditation, which is actually even more restful then sleep.

Be patient in learning to meditate. It could take several months to establish this practice. Twenty minutes of meditation, twice a day, will bring tremendous rewards. Studying *Steps to Knowledge* will give you a solid foundation for building this and other practices that will deepen your experience.

Here you are taking a journey beneath the surface of your mind into deeper states of consciousness. You are building a strong connection to Knowledge, a connection that will stay with you in all circumstances. This will give you strength, clarity and certainty in the increasingly uncertain times ahead.

FOUR PILLARS REVIEW PRACTICE

Take some quiet time each week to review the Four Pillars of your life, remembering that each Pillar is important. Though one may require more effort or attention at any given moment, they are all equally important. Like the four legs of a table, each must be strong. No one Pillar can be sacrificed for the others. You cannot build one to the neglect of all the others, or nothing great can be given to you or realized because you will not have built a strong enough foundation.

THE PILLAR OF RELATIONSHIP

Come to the first Pillar, the Pillar of Relationship, which includes your relationships with people, places, possessions and even with situations and conditions in the world. Feel the condition of this Pillar, the condition of your relationships. Ask within yourself, "Is there anything I need to know about any of my relationships?" Ask this question in such a way that only *yes* or *no* can be the answer. If the answer is *no,* that is fine. Yet if the answer is *yes,* then seek out which relationship this might be. If a relationship comes to mind, ask yourself, "Is there something I need to know here?" Then open yourself to receive what that could be. This may only take a moment, but you must be very present. Insights can come to you during practice or at any time afterwards. What is important is that you are making yourself available to Knowledge and that you have the willingness and readiness to know.

⊰ THE PILLAR OF CAREER AND PROVIDERSHIP ⊱

Now go on to the Pillar of Career and Providership, the Pillar that deals with work, money and contribution in the world. Feel the condition of this Pillar. Continue the same process: "Is there anything I need to know regarding my career and providership in the world?" If something comes to mind, ask yourself, "Is there something I need to know here?" Then open yourself to what that could be. Your insights may come to you in the form of images, ideas, feelings or strong physical sensations, depending upon your individual nature and orientation.

⊰ THE PILLAR OF HEALTH ⊱

Then go on to the Pillar of Health, which includes your physical, mental and emotional health. Feel the condition of this Pillar. Ask yourself, "Is there anything that I need to know about my health or about the health of those who are close to me?" If something comes to mind, ask yourself, "Is there something I need to know here?" If there is, open yourself to it. Face it. Receive it.

⊰ THE PILLAR OF SPIRITUAL DEVELOPMENT ⊱

Then go on to the Pillar of Spiritual Development and feel the condition of this Pillar. Ask yourself, "Is there something I need to know regarding my spiritual development?" And as with all of the other Pillars, if something comes to mind, ask yourself, "Is there something I need to know here?"

THE FOUR PILLARS PRACTICE over time will yield important insights about your life. It is important to record these insights in a journal and review them periodically. Some insights have immediate significance, and others become relevant over time.

As you continue this practice and record your insights, you will see that you really are receiving insights from Knowledge and signs from the world.

In visiting your Four Pillars, take as long as is necessary to complete this process. This will give you the structure you can use to maintain an awareness of these four fundamental areas of your life. As you practice over time, you begin to build, brick by brick, stone by stone, a foundation that the world cannot shake or undermine.

*M*arshall Vian Summers

For the past 25 years, visionary and award-winning author
Marshall Vian Summers has been preparing a New Message for
humanity, which includes a series of writings about the Great
Waves of change. Marshall writes and teaches on a broad
range of subjects related to human evolution, relationships and
spirituality. His writings and recordings are being studied by
growing numbers of people around the world, with translations
in many languages.

Marshall resides with his wife and son in the foothills of
the Rocky Mountains in Colorado. He presents his message to
audiences both in the United States and abroad—a message
that is alarming, profound and ultimately inspiring.